LEGAL LOBBYING: HOW TO MAKE YOUR VOICE HEARD

A Practical Guide to Changing the Law

Mark Kober-Smith
Solicitor and Notary Public

Cavendish
Publishing
Limited

London • Sydney

First published in Great Britain 2000 by Cavendish Publishing Limited,
The Glass House, Wharton Street, London WC1X 9PX, United Kingdom
Telephone: +44 (0)20 7278 8000   Facsimile: +44 (0)20 7278 8080
Email: info@cavendishpublishing.com
Website: www.cavendishpublishing.com

© Kober-Smith, M   2000

British Library Cataloguing and Publication Data

Kober-Smith, Mark
Legal lobbying: how to make your voice heard
1 Lobbying – Great Britain – handbooks, manuals, etc
I Title
328.3'8'0941

ISBN 1 85941 599 7

Printed and bound in Great Britain

A WORD TO THE READER

In this book, I will often portray lobbying as a battle. I see it this way. But I do not want to give the impression that one has to look down on one's opponents, demonise them or, indeed, attribute anything but the best motives to them. It is very difficult for people to act in bad faith, that is, to do things that they consider wrong. Your opponents will consider that they are acting properly, even if your perception is that they are not acting at all.

With regard to my campaign, I want to make it clear that I consider that all my opponents acted at all times in the belief that what they did or argued was in the public interest. The monopoly I was challenging had been created nearly 200 years previously. No government had seriously challenged it. It was for me to convince others that it should be ended. It was no one's duty to agree with me.

Likewise, my own view was and is that the monopoly was in breach of European competition law and that any system of recruitment which relies on apprenticeship tends to restrict numbers and indirectly discriminate against those who do not have contacts in the profession. However, this is simply my opinion, and does not in any way imply that plumbers, solicitors, Scriveners or barristers actually intend to discriminate against anyone. Similarly, my interpretation of EU law is simply that, one person's view. Others are free to disagree with me. Many did!

ACKNOWLEDGMENTS

I would like to thank everyone who has been kind enough to give me their help, whether by way of constructive criticism of the book or simply bearing with me in listening to my arguments for the abolition of the Scrivener monopoly. Without their help, I would have blundered on, but timely comments and suggestions have helped me greatly in focusing attention.

In particular, I would like to thank Granville Hodge, Solicitor of Cluff, Hodge & Co and my work colleagues at my then firm, Prince Evans, Solicitors. I would especially thank Philip Eldin-Taylor (who revised the key letter to MPs) and Gavin Heighton, who gave many suggestions and continual support.

Amongst others who supported me, I would single out Martin Green PhD (who would be the best lobbyist in the country if he decided to put his energies in that direction), who supported me from the beginning with many valuable suggestions; Andrew Ayodeji-Dodd; Mark Martin; and my ever-efficient secretary, Kalwinder Matharu (whose help in getting out the letters to MPs was invaluable). I would also like to thank Neil Bartlett for his suggestions. Special thanks are also due to Jon Lloyd and Jo Reddy at Cavendish Publishing for their help in getting this book completed.

I thank my parents for teaching me how to persist and how to argue a case, and my father for his understanding of human nature and the help that has been to me.

Lastly, I thank my wife, Anémone, for her intellectual analysis and endless patience.

Of course, although many people have helped me, responsibility for any faults in the book rests with me.

CONTENTS

INTRODUCTION AND AIM OF THE BOOK

A man was asked if he knew how to play the piano. 'I don't know', he said. 'What do you mean, you don't know?', they asked. 'I never tried.'

Anecdote.

INTRODUCTION

This book is about how one person, or a few, can change the law and how I, and three other people, did it.

It is intended as a guide for the busy person who wants to change the law, but does not know where to start.

The book contains in its appendices sources of information for the campaigner and guides to where to find help.

When I started my campaign, I had no supporters, no experience of lobbying at all and no knowledge of how to do it. The book relates how I moved from a situation in which only I wanted the change to one in which change was supported by (amongst others): the Liberal Democrats; the Conservative Party; the Law; the Office of Fair Trading; the Commission for Racial Equality; the Equal Opportunities Commission; Stonewall; many Labour MPs; and the Lord Chancellor. My change came into force on 1 November 1999.

RELEVANCE TO THE READER

It is true that this book is highly influenced by my specific campaign. It may be hard to initially see the relevance of my struggle to yours. The key is this: nobody is as interested in your campaign as you are. The powers that be are happy with the way things are. Their starting point is to keep them that way and to ignore your campaign as wrong headed, irrelevant or of such a low priority that action can be postponed to an appropriate time – that is, never.

The weak point of my campaign – its obscurity – is its strength. The fact that, initially, I had no support at all from anyone means that you, the reader, cannot be starting from a worse position. You, like me, have nowhere to go but up.

The book moves from the specific facts of the campaign, its planning and strategy, to general considerations about how to apply these principles in other situations.

AIM OF THE BOOK

This book is primarily aimed at the smaller group or individual. The aim is to give people the confidence to act and win, even without a large network. But the book can be used by any lobbyist and the appendices review the key literature on the subject.

Some campaigns do involve large organisations. For example, the books of Des Wilson, who won significant victories in many campaigns (for example, in the successful campaign to phase out lead in petrol) are referred to, along with those of other experienced lobbyists, in Appendix 5.

MY APPROACH – LOBBYING AS GAME PLAYING

Lobbying is a simple process – it is asking people to do what you want. Since they often say 'no', the trick is to turn that no into a 'yes'. In a way, lobbying is like chess or other games of strategy. You have to guess what the other side will do and try to outwit or outmanoeuvre them. Sometimes, of course, people are delighted to help you. I am immensely grateful to those who have done this and I hope to be able to acknowledge them through the course of this book.

It involves psychology, timing and a sense of what other people are trying to achieve, so that you can be aware of it when planning your campaign.

Lobbying can move from being exhilarating to wearying and boring in moments. The point to remember is that it is a game played for real stakes. You have to be aware that your victory is usually defeat for someone else. Time spent by the authorities on your issue (for example, getting your Bill passed through Parliament) is time lost for someone else. You will probably make more enemies than friends. You have to be ruthless as well as persistent. However, I am assuming that you have decided that you must achieve your goal and I turn now to the question of beginning.

CHAPTER 2

BEGINNING

A journey of a thousand miles begins with a single step.

Chinese proverb.

We spend 70% of our time wondering whether to act, only 30% acting.

The author.

BEGINNING

Beginning can be hard and finishing harder. Yet, the key to success is the belief that one should and will win.

It is true that all campaigns have their unique slant and each involves different issues. Some will involve massive letter writing campaigns, press appearances and demonstrations. Others will be almost invisible to the general public and yet just as effective. It is the second type with which this book is concerned.

However, I suggest that the will to win is crucial in both. The will to win has three effects:

- first, it keeps you going when the outlook is bleak;
- secondly, it sends a signal to your subconscious that it must work to provide you with ideas and help when needed. You become always on the alert for information that can help you;
- thirdly, the strength of your resolve is always tested by those opposing you. If decision makers did what you asked immediately, there would be no point in writing this book. *Conversely, once the people you are up against realise that you are not going away, now or ever, until your cause is won, their perceptions of you and the issues start to change. You have become a factor in the decision making process simply by refusing to go away. The next step is pushing the decision your way.*

THE BACKGROUND TO MY STORY

I qualified as a solicitor in November 1990. I had come to the law as a mature student and had become keen on study, as many mature students are. I had completed my first degree, then taken a conversion course to become a solicitor, then been apprenticed, in the customary way, to an existing solicitor in the firm I worked at in London. That apprenticeship lasted for two years, ending in late 1990. During my articles, I had studied for and passed a degree in French and a Diploma in Translation from French to English. I had the formal qualifications to be a professional translator.

As it happened, the law firm I worked for was in the City of London. I was interested in the legal profession as a whole and noticed that, in England and Wales, the most ancient legal professions were: solicitors; barristers; and notaries public.

In addition to these three, there were legal executives and licensed conveyancers. Licensed conveyancers specialised in conveyancing. Legal executives had a much broader role and could do most work a solicitor could. Typically, legal executives were secretaries who took a series of law exams while working full time in a law office.

Legal executives and licensed conveyancers were often highly skilled lawyers. Yet, in the hierarchy of the legal professions, they stood as newcomers. You could move from either profession to be a solicitor or notary public, but further examinations and training were needed. The licensed conveyancers and legal executives played a part in this story, but, for now, I will concentrate on the oldest legal professions.

TYPES OF LAWYERS

- *Solicitors*, like myself, had tended always to deal with the preparation of contracts and the drafting of other legal documents. However, many of them were also involved in work in the courts. Indeed, they did most of the representation of defendants in the lowest courts and a fair amount in the county courts, the next highest level in the court hierarchy. This amounted to some 90% of all advocacy. But they had, until very recently, been prevented from appearing as advocates in the higher courts. Although, for example, they prepared the papers for court, interviewed the witnesses and managed the enormous amount of paperwork that could be generated by a case, they had been barred from actually pleading their client's case before higher courts, such as the High Court, the Court of Appeal or the House of Lords. In 1990, there were roughly 65,000 solicitors in practice.

- *Barristers* wore wigs and appeared as advocates in court, arguing the case on behalf of the client, largely following the instructions of the solicitor in charge of the case. They could appear in any court of the land without restriction. They could also give legal advice and draft legal documents, just like solicitors. Since their rules of professional practice forbade them to take instructions directly from the public, they tended to concentrate on court work. In 1990, there were approximately 7,000 of them in practice.

- *Notaries public* were a small group, numbering only around 1,000. Nearly 970 of these were also solicitors. They were not involved with litigation at all. Their role was completely undefined by statute but, according to the legal textbooks, was otherwise potentially as wide ranging as that of either solicitors or barristers. They were entitled, like barristers or solicitors, to draw up legal documents or act as conveyancers in the buying and selling of property. Their work had a lot of contact with people with overseas connections, since the office of notary, as we shall see, has a great deal of importance in many countries.

THE MONOPOLY AND ME

I found that I could quite easily become a notary public, since my studies to become a solicitor exempted me from most of the examinations. I could then practise anywhere in England and Wales, with one major exception – I could not practise in London.

I worked in the City of London and I found out that, to be a notary there, one had to first become a member of the Worshipful Company of Scriveners. Access to the profession in London was still governed by the Public Notaries Act 1801. One had to be articled for five years to an existing London notary who was a member of the Company. I decided to ring up the few firms of notaries and ask them if I could do this.

The reply was the same from each. There were no vacancies and none were anticipated for at least five years. I was disappointed, but let the matter drop. It was only some years later, in 1995, that I found myself considering the issue again. The more I examined the issue, the more nonsensical the matter seemed. How could it be the case that I could practise as a notary in Manchester or Surrey, but not in London? How could I be perfectly competent in Berkshire, but banned in the heart of the capital? I decided that there was no justification for the monopoly and that it should be ended. The question was how.

THE PROBLEM TO BE SOLVED – A NEED FOR RESEARCH

I decided to analyse the situation and decide who could or should help me. I would use a multi-pronged attack, since a quick look at the opposing forces convinced me that I would find few allies. I could not rely on any one approach to get me what I wanted. I thought the best way to defeat my enemy was to understand his approach and to be able to articulate the opponent's arguments better than he could.

I think I can best illustrate this by showing the results of my research. I reasoned that my need was to be able to convince people of my case by being able to summarise it succinctly and whenever I could.

THE PROFESSION OF NOTARY PUBLIC FROM ROMAN TIMES UNTIL NOW

Roman times

My starting point was the legal reference works and the key book on the profession of notary public, *Brooke's Notary*. I was very interested to see that the current edition was edited by Nigel Ready, a notary member of the Worshipful Company of Scriveners. I thought this was something which would probably prove very useful to me.

The profession traces its origin to Roman times.[1] Notaries then were professional scribes, who set up shop in the market place. They drew up deeds on behalf of members of the public who applied to them. Once signed, attested by witnesses and duly authenticated by an official seal, the act or deed became binding on all parties to it.

The profession survived the fall of the Roman empire. In the 12th century, the formal study of Roman law enjoyed a renaissance in Italy. At Bologna, medieval jurists began to claim that the deeds drawn up by notaries were not simply ordinary legal documents. They asserted that they were public documents and thus especially to be trusted. From that time, legal documents came to be classed as essentially one of two types:

(a) private instruments – simply drawn up between the parties concerned, possibly witnessed by others;

(b) notarial instruments in public form – drawn up by a notary.

The significance of having the document drawn up by the notary was that greater credence was attached to a document drawn up by a notary. A notary was under a duty to make a faithful record of matters brought to him. A private document could have been drawn up by anyone, including people having no such duty.

On the continent of Europe, then, in those countries strongly influenced by Roman law, the notary became the most trusted and important of all lawyers.

---

1   For this account of the history of the notarial profession, I have drawn on material in Chapter 1 of *Brooke's Notary*, 1992, Sweet & Maxwell, pp 1–19.

The consolidation of notarial power after the French Revolution

In France, after the French Revolution, notaries were briefly abolished. They were brought back under Napoleon. The success of Napoleon's campaigns in Belgium, the Netherlands, Italy and Spain, to name only a few countries, led to the adoption of a system of law in those countries, which was largely based on the French Civil Code. The Civil Code systematised all French law and preserved an important place for notaries. It became essential to use a notary to record the majority of important property transactions. If you wanted to sell your property, or even give it away, you needed to have a notary draw up the deed of transfer. Failure to do so would not invalidate your decision as between yourself and your buyer. On the death of the seller, however, the seller's children could deny that transfer or ownership had taken place, since the proper formalities had not been observed.

Since the Civil Code prescribed that many acts must be done before a notary, notaries were never short of work. Additionally, most European countries retained the idea that there must only be a limited number of notaries and each notary would be confined to one geographical area. Notaries could become very rich, since they had a job for life, no competitors and charged fees according to the value of the property transferred.

I use the past tense but, largely, the same picture applies today. Notaries in continental Europe are still largely administering an updated version of Napoleon's Civil Code. They continue to have jobs for life, no real competitors and they continue to charge according to the value of the property transferred.

I noted from this that there was potentially a lot at stake here and abroad.

THE ENGLISH EXCEPTION AND THE BEGINNING OF THE SCRIVENER MONOPOLY

Notaries in England tended to be appointed by the Pope. This was because (although they drafted documents just like their continental counterparts) the English courts gave no particular credence to the documents produced by notaries. Then, as now, the central principle was that if evidence was to be given, it should be done in person. The court would decide who to believe and would not give one kind of document precedence over any other kind.

Church courts existed alongside the common law courts and notaries could work there. The connection with the Pope was severed at the time of the English Reformation under Henry VIII, but English notaries today are still all nominally appointed by the Archbishop of Canterbury, who took over all the functions previously carried out under Papal authority.

Notaries stayed busy as private lawyers and the original connection with the church began to loosen. *Brooke's Notary* records that, by the 14th century, there was a strong connection between the profession of notary and the Company of Scriveners. This became so much so that: 'In 1373, the Scriveners of the City of London formed themselves into a company, for the purpose of preserving to themselves a monopoly of the activities of their profession. From then ... members of the Company of Scriveners enjoyed within the City of London and a circuit of three miles of the City a monopoly of the "art or mystery" of preparing all deeds, charters and other writings which, by the common law or custom of this realm, required to be confirmed or attested by a seal.'[2]

Brooke's Notary records in a footnote to this quotation that 'in those days, all writings intended to have legal effect were under seal'.[3]

I was both amused and fascinated to discover that a monopoly granted in 1373 was still in force today. I was pleased to see that *Brooke's Notary* was so direct about the motive for the formation of the Scriveners Company – that is, to get the benefit of the monopoly. I thought this would be useful later.

Struggles with other lawyers

The present division of the legal professions in England dates back no earlier than the early 19th century. The profession of solicitor was merely one of many, all more or less in competition with each other. There were attorneys, solicitors, proctors, notaries, sergeants-at-law and barristers.

Naturally, London was a prime site for legal work. Since the Scrivener monopoly was one of effectively all legal work which did not involve litigation (since they claimed a monopoly of the right to draw up deeds, the only valid legal document) and since the monopoly covered nearly all of London, there was bound to be a battle. It appears that the Scriveners tried to have their monopoly enforced in 1760, by suing an attorney called Smith. They alleged he was infringing their sole rights to draw up deeds.

THE END OF THE FIRST SCRIVENER MONOPOLY AND THE START OF THE NEW MONOPOLY

The Scriveners lost the case and London became open for legal business. Yet, in 1801, they succeeded in having a Bill passed through Parliament which provided that, if one was to practise as a notary in the City of London or a

---

2   *Brooke's Notary*, 1992, Sweet & Maxwell, p 14.
3   *Ibid*, p 14, fn 42.

circuit of three miles of the City, one first had to become a member of the Scriveners Company.

Since one could now draw up legal documents in that area as a solicitor or barrister, it seems that the law was not strongly opposed. The new law also provided that, within a radius of 10 miles of Mansion House (situated in the centre of the City of London), only a certain special category of notaries could be appointed and, in practice, very few were.

Indeed, few Scrivener notaries were ever appointed. *Brooke's Notary* recorded that, in 1884, there had been 33 Scrivener notaries. In 1995, there were 30 and it seemed the numbers had been much the same over the last 100 years.[4]

In effect, the Scrivener notaries not only had an exclusive monopoly in London, but they had only half a dozen competitors within 10 miles of London. This led to inconvenience for the public, since the area up to 10 miles around London was huge in size, population and consequent legal needs. There was pressure for reform.

THE COURTS AND LEGAL SERVICES ACT 1990

There had been increasing criticism of the archaic restrictive practices of the legal professions throughout the 1980s. Solicitors were criticised for the fact that the fees they charged for conveyancing were based on the value of the property and not solely on the amount of work they had done. Barristers were criticised by solicitors for not allowing them to act as advocates in the higher courts. The public felt that lawyers were overpaid and underworked.

Their monopolies, restrictive practices and high fees seemed ripe for the introduction of competition. The Conservative Government in power at the time was strongly free market in outlook. Eventually, it introduced a Bill which became law as the Courts and Legal Services Act 1990.

The Act removed the statutory monopoly barristers had over advocacy in the higher courts. This historic advance for solicitors was tempered by the fact that a committee of judges (practically all ex-barristers) set the conditions for the aptitude test for solicitors wishing to exercise these advocacy rights. Many solicitors felt that the conditions were too stringent, more stringent than they were for barristers. This slowed the rate at which solicitors could qualify as advocates.

Solicitors were made subject to further competition in their most profitable area, conveyancing. The Act set up a new profession of licensed conveyancer. This was to give the public a choice of which profession to use.

---

4   *Brooke's Notary*, 1992, Sweet & Maxwell, p 19.

NOTARIES – CHANGE – BUT THE
SCRIVENER MONOPOLY REMAINS

Prior to 1990, most notaries had only been allowed to practise in a defined geographical area. If you were appointed a notary in Manchester, you could not be one in Leeds. Since you could only become a notary by being articled to one, pockets of notaries developed.

You might have three notaries in one law firm in one town and none for 50 miles around.

The Courts and Legal Services Act did several things:

- it abolished the idea of separate geographical 'patches', meaning that notaries could now take their skills to different areas;
- it allowed for qualification by examination, so that people could become notaries without working for someone who already was one;
- it effectively abolished the 10 mile 'exclusion zone' around the City of London by abolishing the special class of notaries who could practise there;
- it specifically reaffirmed the Scrivener monopoly area of three miles in the City of London and three miles around its boundaries.

All of these points, save the last, helped my case. The puzzle was how Scrivener notaries had managed to keep their monopoly when both barristers and solicitors had lost theirs.

I realised I had an uphill struggle. Looking at *Hansard*, I found that the abolition of the monopoly had not even been discussed. I concluded that either:

(a) the Scriveners were very good at lobbying; or

(b) nobody cared about the issue; or

(c) both.

SUMMARY OF MY RESEARCH

The results of my research were that:

- the Scriveners had a monopoly and few had ever qualified to join them;
- I noted that the seeming limitation on numbers appeared to be an equivalent of the continental system of *numerus clausus*, that is, a control on entry which had the fortunate side effect (at least for those benefiting from it) of reducing competition and probably increasing fees. Whether this limitation was consciously imposed or not was impossible to say;

- there was an interesting European angle. Could I or other would-be notaries qualify as an English notary and then claim rights to practise in Europe? Could foreign notaries practise in England and, if not, why not?;
- the Courts and Legal Services Act 1990 had been passed after consultation with the legal professions. Had anyone objected to the monopoly and what had the Government done about these objections? It did not appear likely that there was any clamour for the abolition of the monopoly, since, otherwise, it would surely have gone;
- did domestic or international law against anti-competitive practices apply to the monopoly? Could I argue that the monopoly must be removed to fulfil these legal obligations?;
- what about the seeming tight limits on numbers admitted to the Scriveners Company? Could I argue that these limits were illegal or potentially discriminatory?;
- what was the actual justification for the monopoly? *Brooke's Notary* was interesting, in that it did not deal with this issue directly. It suggested, I felt, that Scrivener notaries were superior to other notaries. This seemed, however, to be irrelevant even if it were true. No doubt, solicitors felt superior to licensed conveyancers, but they still had to suffer competition from them.

I decided that I would have to start making a public noise about the issue and see where all the actors in the drama were situated.

GENERAL POINTS

- I suggested that thorough analysis of the issues is a sound basis for the rest of the campaign. In particular, I found that works written by your opponents are the best evidence. They cannot deny their own words and your interpretation of what they have said or written can attack them on the facts they themselves have admitted.
- The issue for me was to widen the case from 'why can't I practise as a notary in the City of London?', an issue that concerned only me, to why such a monopoly could be tolerated. I saw that the issue was minor in appearance, but could also be seen as a key issue of principle. At present, the monopoly was not even a minor issue; it was a non-issue. I had to make it an issue.
- In every area, there is always somebody whose job it is to do something about it. Once they have been identified, one can go into action. If the issue is dirty streets, the responsible party is the local government. If it is dirty air, the Government is responsible along with local government. Finding out who should be acting is a key step. Often, responsibility is passed

around, like a grenade with the pin pulled out. It has to be made to stop somewhere.

- I decided that I would find quite a few people who were responsible and stir up the issue as much as possible. I made a decision that my case would be acted on only when enough people got bothered by it. I decided to bother many.

- The key point was to push the issue out into the public domain. I wanted to get into the newspapers, in order to make decision makers realise that they had a potential public embarrassment on their hands if action was not taken.

- I decided to find and approach all the key players to work out where they stood, whether any of them were likely to act and whether they would support me. The reader will see my analysis of this in the next chapter.

CHAPTER 3

WHO ARE THE PLAYERS?

A committee is a device for avoiding decision making.

Popular wisdom.

WHO ARE THE PLAYERS?

If we look at lobbying as a game (the goal being to get our law passed), then we need to see where everybody is in the game and what their objectives and fears are. Then, we can phrase the arguments that will convince them either to help us or refrain from hindering us.

The players are, in every case:

- the Government;
- the Civil Service;
- the people affected by any decision, either as members of the general public or otherwise;
- the professionals or others directly affected. For example, greater regulation of taxi drivers affects taxi drivers directly, but is aimed at protecting the general public;
- the media;
- other political parties;
- any lobby groups active in that field;
- national legal obligations;
- international legal obligations.

THE INTERACTION OF THE PLAYERS

Every campaign will be different. Some lobbying campaigns will be able to rely on huge letter writing campaigns and committed media support. Others will be very small scale. Yet, I suggest that a simple formula for summarising the immense complexity of the potential interactions between the Government, the public and all the above players is this:

The more the Government can be persuaded that it will lose by not supporting you and gain from supporting you, the more likely it is you will get Government support and your law passed.

The Government decision making process is roughly as follows:

- the Government will take the decision to pass a law after taking advice from the Civil Service;

- the Civil Service will have sifted and reviewed the submissions and likely reactions of the people regarded as being most affected by the decision. It will also consider the legal position of the Government, both in relation to existing national legislation and European Union (EU) law and international Treaty obligations. Many proposals from lobbyists will not even make it to scrutiny by the Government, however, since they will be effectively shelved by civil servants screening their minister from having to make too many decisions. This danger can be sidestepped;

- the Government will weigh the advice from its civil servants against its own political agenda, that of its opponents and the possibility of gain or loss for itself in the eyes of the media, the public and its supporters.

Of course, there is no such thing as a government, simply an agglomeration of individuals. Getting through to the relevant minister proved vital in my campaign, but the process of decision making is basically as set out above.

THE AIM OF THE GAME – TO PASS A LAW

How can this be done? There are two basic methods:

(a) a Private Member's Bill passed on a free vote of the Commons;

(b) a Government sponsored Bill or clause.

Ultimately, we can only change the law if enough decision makers support the move to do so. Sometimes, that can be MPs directly, as in the passing of a Private Member's Bill. This has led to significant reforms, such as David Steel MP's Bill to legalise abortion, or the bills to legalise homosexuality and abolish the death penalty for murder. However, Parliamentary time is always limited and it is doubtful if any of these Bills would have become law without the tacit support of the Government of the day.

Furthermore, there is an increasing tendency for Private Member's Bills simply to be another opportunity for the Government to get one of its own Bills passed in another guise. (For discussion of parliamentary procedure on the passing of Bills, see Appendices 3 and 4.)

The most likely route is therefore going to be the Government sponsored Bill or clause. I was often invited to put forward a Private Member's Bill, but I always declined. This is because:

(a) the Government sponsored Bill or clause has a much greater chance of succeeding; and

(b) sometimes, a change in the law is not enough on its own. You need to have the Government and its advisers think as you do, so that they will then act to forestall problems or blockages that may arise as a result of the change you have promoted.

THE ROLE OF THE CIVIL SERVICE

One of the key points noted by commentators on the political system is that each government relies greatly on advice provided by its civil servants. This is not to say that the civil service has its own view on all issues, imposed willy-nilly on incoming governments, *Yes, Minister* style. It is simply that governments are transient and ministers even more so. Someone has to be continuously aware of what the issues are in any area, so that ministers can receive advice. That someone is the Civil Service.

Yet, the Civil Service itself relies on feedback and opinions. Each civil servant, at any level in the decision making process, has a lot of files to deal with. It is impossible to become expert at them all. So, arguments submitted by people who are affected by their decisions can have a significant impact on the advice they give to ministers and the consequent direction of government policy. For example, in deciding whether or not to reform the teaching profession, ministers will take account not only of any manifesto promises, but also of a general duty to consult. They will ask the civil service to prepare a report on the current state of the teaching profession, the proposals for change and the likely reactions of those affected. A civil servant or a group will compile the report, after reviewing submissions from the teaching unions, experts in the field, previous Civil Service reports in the same area and so on.

The impact of advice

I suggest that the advice ultimately received by the minister, and the statements made in Parliament about an issue by that minister, are affected very clearly by this input from outside. Indeed, surely, this is part of what democracy is about.

I can sympathise with those who deplore the closed nature of this debate. Not many people know that you can make submissions of your case. It is also wrong that it is very difficult to find who you can make them to. I am personally in favour of a strong and effective Freedom of Information Act, but it is curious to see often how few people use the existing processes.

For example, many solicitors have criticised the monopoly of rights of advocacy held by barristers. Yet, when the Lord Chancellor decided to open the issue up for public consultation, there were only three individual solicitors who wrote in with their views. Rights of advocacy will now be easier for solicitors to obtain, but instead of, rather than because of, their representations. Of course, in this case, the Law Society made submissions on behalf of solicitors.

An almost judicial role

The Civil Service has to balance all issues and make a recommendation. Since its overview also needs to take into account existing government legal obligations, then many campaigns can be brought within this remit. The campaign for lead free petrol was greatly strengthened by the fact that the Government's own advisers were suggesting a significant risk to health and Government policy was, of course, to promote health.

In making submissions to the Civil Service, I think it is vital to maintain a policy of absolute honesty, to the extent of making people aware of the flaws in your own arguments. Apart from the fact that this seems to be the only ethical thing to do, it is also more effective. It is better to point out yourself the weaker points of your case and deal with them, rather than assume that they will not be noticed.

MOTIVATION OF THE CIVIL SERVICE

The official task of the civil service is to carry out Government policy. Since this can frequently change, even between elections, a kind of 'civil service view' emerges, which I would summarise as follows:

- *if it ain't broke, don't fix it* – since there is more to do than can be done, matters which can wait should be left. In the private sector, this is known as time management or prioritisation of tasks. It is a vital skill. At any one time, there can only be a relatively limited number of files actively being progressed. The point is to make sure yours is one of them;

- *if your minister or the Government prioritises the matter, it has to be prioritised* – there are specific guidelines on how quickly letters should be answered, for example. Ministers get the quickest replies; the public, the slowest. The intervention of an MP speeds up the response to a letter from a member of the public;

- *embarrassment to the Government and the Civil Service is to be avoided and files have to be managed (that is, kept under control)* – basically, effective file management means keeping the file out of the public domain, whether that is the political realm or the courts. If there is a strong risk of legal action or many MPs become involved in the issue, the file swiftly moves up the prioritisation list;

- *files should be dealt with fairly* – it is vital to realise that civil servants, on the whole, want to get their job done and do it well. Since there is nearly always someone who should be dealing with your file, you need to find them and help them to deal with it.

All the other players

I propose to deal with the other players with reference to my specific campaign.

PLAYERS IN THE NOTARY PUBLIC WORLD

Administration of the Profession – the Faculty Office and the Master of the Faculties

The profession of notary public was a small world, with an antiquated feel to it. Notaries were still appointed by the Archbishop of Canterbury. Each notary, when appointed, was granted a Faculty, or authority to act, by the Archbishop. Of course, in practice, he delegated this responsibility to the Faculty Office, an organisation looking after various aspects of the work and duties of the Archbishop. It was headed by the Master of the Faculties, a High Court judge appointed to look after the legal matters which still fell under the jurisdiction of the Archbishop.

In turn, the Master of the Faculties was advised by the notarial profession and its representatives. Prominent amongst his advisors were the Scrivener notaries. The examinations set for Scrivener notaries were set and marked by Scrivener notaries. The examinations set for non-Scrivener notaries were also set and marked by Scrivener notaries. A Scrivener notary was the editor of the main textbook on notarial practice and the Master of the Faculties was clearly of the opinion that Scrivener notaries were better than other notaries. He had said as much in a judgment he had given in his court, the Court of Faculties.

The Master was also advised by the Registrar of the Court of Faculties, who dealt with day to day administration from the Faculty Office. The Registrar was a solicitor and his firm was well known for its work in ecclesiastical law. Telephone discussions with the Faculty Office made me consider that its view was conservative. The status quo was to be preserved, because it was the current status quo. Any change needed to come from the Government.

Therefore, I did not expect much support from the Master for abolition of the monopoly, nor indeed from the Archbishop of Canterbury or the Faculty

Office. Of course, since my aim was to create as much noise as possible, that did not stop me from trying.

THE PROFESSIONAL ORGANISATIONS REPRESENTING NOTARIES

The Worshipful Company of Scriveners

The Scriveners were a City livery company. Becoming a member of the Company gave you the freedom of the City of London. It was a privilege granted to few. It carried with it the right to vote in elections for aldermen who, in turn, were and are the only people who vote to elect the Mayor of the City of London.

Originally, the livery companies were guilds, groups of craftsmen who had banded together to share knowledge and companionship and to raise the price of their labour. This last objective was largely achieved by:

(a) making membership of the guild a precondition of working in the craft; and

(b) keeping down the number of members.

Long before Adam Smith, the guilds had understood that high demand and short supply means higher prices.

The guilds had arisen in medieval times and their power had once been massive within each trade or calling. However, it had gradually faded, not least because the City of London had ceased to be an area where the crafts were practised. In the 14th century, haberdashers, cheesemakers and cordwainers (which all still exist as livery companies) plied a profitable trade in the City. Now, manufacturing trades had moved elsewhere.

Manufacturing had been replaced by financial services and lawyers. The City was a more attractive area than ever for a notary. Of course, I would not suggest that the present day Scriveners wished to keep out competitors as the earliest Scriveners had. They simply wished, as they saw it, to keep up standards and protect the public.

However, I thought it a little unlikely that the Scriveners Company would ask for abolition of the monopoly. Yet, many aspects of the Company were open to attack. Amongst these, I noted:

- it was a contradiction (in an open society based on merit and achievement) for access to a profession to be dependent on membership of a medieval guild;

- the area covered by the monopoly, (the City of London and three miles around it) was exactly the same as in 1373. A lot had happened since then;

- the absurdly antiquated practices of the law are a favourite theme of the media. I thought that I would be able to get publicity for my campaign on the back of this. So it proved;

- members of City livery companies tended to be white, male and middle class. I thought that this raised the possibility of indirect discrimination against women or minorities. Since this, thankfully, was no longer acceptable, I thought that I could use this fact against them. I would argue that perpetuation of the monopoly would tend to perpetuate this indirect discrimination. Of course, the possibility of indirect discrimination does not mean that any Scrivener, or the guild itself, had any intent to discriminate. It is simply that people tend to recruit people like themselves and this tends to give less chances to those outside the loop;

- even the notarial textbook could not reasonably argue that notaries in London formed a separate profession. This would mean that there were only 30 members of the entire profession. Yet, if the London notaries were members of the same profession as notaries from outside London, how could provincial notaries be denied access to the London market on any logical grounds? One would have to argue either that other notaries were incompetent or that the monopoly was simply a historical fact, which could not be questioned. Most likely, you would keep as silent as possible, since this was the best way to avoid debate. Of course, I had no idea what Scriveners actually did think. I simply could not see any other arguments for keeping the monopoly.

I decided to research the Scriveners closely and to start a debate which would force their arguments into the open. Once this was done, I could defeat them intellectually. It would then be a question of terminating the monopoly in practice.

The Notaries' Society

This represented nearly all the remaining notaries in England and Wales who practised outside of the Scrivener monopoly area. It was headed by a Council which, traditionally, contained members from all areas of England and Wales.

Virtually all notaries had qualified under the system of five years' apprenticeship ('articles') to an existing notary. They were also used to the pre-1990 system, in which notaries had been appointed to practice only in a particular area and very few were appointed in all. So, local monopolies were something they had grown up with and accepted. The Scrivener monopoly was simply another example of this.

Additionally, notaries from other regions of the country often did not aspire to moving to London. Therefore, the problems of London notaries were not a priority. By far the majority of their income came from their practice as solicitors. Notarial income per notary outside of the larger cities was generally less than £5,000 per annum.

The Notaries' Society largely reflected the indifference of most of its members. The Society was neutral on the question of whether the Scrivener monopoly should be abolished.

In practice, I felt that this neutrality ended up as support for the Scriveners (since not opposing the monopoly, in my view, meant supporting it). I decided to push the Society on the question of whether the professional standards of its members were as high as those of Scriveners. Since they could hardly castigate their own members, I would then use this statement of equivalence of standards as one of the key points of my attack on the monopoly. After all, if 1,000 notaries thought they were as good as Scriveners, who was I to argue?

SIDELINING THE 'NEUTRALS'

More generally, I thought that the Notaries' Society and the Faculty Office were bodies that could be sidelined when votes were counted. Since they were always officially neutral, they would not be able to come to the support of the Scriveners in public. Once I could get the debate into the public arena, their neutrality would become a comfort. I would be able to announce that the organisation representing 97% of notaries were not against abolition and neither was the body regulating the profession.

The debate would then be a simple one: Scriveners on the one hand; and me, and anyone else I could muster, on the other. Put like that, I was already in front. I could imagine getting quite a few allies. I could not see the Scriveners finding anyone to speak up for them.

The Association of Solicitor Notaries of Greater London (the ASN)

This was a group of approximately 35 solicitor notaries practising around London. The founder was Hans Hartwig, who wished to practise as a notary in the Scrivener monopoly area and was engaged in litigation with the Faculty Office to this end.

The ASN was not a party to the litigation and was not actively campaigning for the end of the monopoly. Its members were, however, clearly against the monopoly. It simply comprised a group of notaries working near London who came together from time to time for educational talks and discussion about notarial matters.

A common feeling among ASN members was that the Notaries' Society was too remote and did not give much priority to the problems of London based notaries, who were the only notaries to directly suffer from the Scrivener monopoly.

I decided that the ASN was a good source of potential contacts, but how keen people would be to actually do something to end the monopoly was uncertain. Although most ASN members were clearly against the monopoly, they, like other notaries, were much busier as solicitors. So, allocating a lot of time to trying to gain more notarial work did not make any clear economic sense.

Ending the monopoly, many reasoned, would not necessarily lead to more work for themselves. The large City of London law firms would probably benefit most, since they were physically closer to City clients and could see them quickest. Indeed, once the monopoly was ended, the cake would simply be sliced a great many more times. The Scriveners would lose out, but so would everyone else.

The most lucrative option would be to oblige the Scriveners to admit a few new members, but continue to exclude others. This would be done on the basis that some notaries (that is, some solicitor notaries in Greater London), through long experience, had gained the right of admission to the elite. I was against this, since I was in the process of qualifying as a notary. For me, the only fair method of selection inside London was the one used outside London, no less but, certainly, no more. This was by examinations open to all.

I decided that I would receive only limited help from the ASN. I would have to create a situation in which selective admission to work in London was no longer feasible.

The Law Society

The Law Society represented solicitors but, in my view, not very well. It had failed to gain many advantages for solicitors and indeed had not been able to defend the monopoly solicitors had effectively had over conveyancing. Yet, since nearly all solicitors were notaries, I thought that the Law Society had a duty to take up a matter of importance to solicitor notaries like me – that is, the monopoly. If it did, the impact for the credibility of my campaign would be enormous. The balance sheet for the 'those for and against the monopoly' vote would suddenly show an extra 65,000 people on the 'against' side, that being the number of solicitors spoken for by the Law Society.

The problem was that I was one person from a small firm. It is not perhaps generally realised, but certainly, until the last few years, I think it would be fair to say that the Law Society had been run by the large City firms of solicitors for their own interests. The income from notarial work, large though it could be for a small firm or individual, was minuscule when compared to the massive legal bills City firms regularly charged for their work as solicitors.

Since those running the Law Society would therefore not prioritise the matter, I simply needed the Law Society to flush out the arguments of the Scriveners and to support abolition as a matter of principle. I did not realise how difficult this would be.

THE GOVERNMENT

I started the campaign under the Conservative Government, in July 1995. Victory came in February 1999, under the new Labour administration.

The Conservatives, both in and out of office, believed in competition as the essence of a free market. At least, that is what the official line was, to which there were often exceptions. They believed that the invisible hand of the market would ensure that the consumer would benefit from competition and receive, as a result, goods and services which were cheaper, better and more adapted to consumer requirements.

As mentioned earlier, the Conservative Government had decided to remove barriers to competition in the field of legal services by the passing of the Courts and Legal Services Act 1990. This had not been painless, since many of its own supporters were fervent supporters of the free market only when competition was imposed on other people. In short, it was good to have competition for air fares or the price of beer, but bad to have it for barristers and solicitors. However, the Act had been passed regardless.

Yet, the Scriveners had escaped abolition and no one knew why. *Hansard* did not record that the issue had even been discussed in Parliament. On the face of it, this seemed a crushing blow. It was very unlikely that the Government would revisit the question of reforming the legal professions again. Once in the lifetime of a Parliament was quite enough in terms of parliamentary time.

I will return to the question of competition for time later on. The key point is that each minister normally has a wish list of Bills that he or she would like to see get passed into law. Not all can be satisfied, since time is short. Although the more senior and powerful ministers have a greater chance of getting parliamentary time for legislation, to do so is always a battle. Therefore, going back to pass additional Acts to remedy the defects of the first Bill you passed is highly unlikely, unless the damage that would otherwise be done is large.

I thought of this when my amendment to abolish the monopoly failed to make it into the Access to Justice Bill under the new Labour Government. I decided that I had to get Labour to decide to add my amendment there and then. Labour would not revisit the issue and the Scriveners' monopoly would remain for many more years.

LABOUR AND CONSERVATIVES – A DUAL STRATEGY

Labour had essentially the same philosophy of competition as the Conservatives. It too believed that the public should have the benefits of greater choice and had talked a lot about this in opposition, even publishing policy proposals, but notaries had escaped their attention altogether.

I decided that the Government should be pressed on its principles. If it believed in competition, why was it so restricted as regards notarial services in the City of London? This could be a stick for Labour to beat the Conservatives with. Further, raising the issue with the Government would mean that some civil servant, somewhere, would be allocated the question of notaries and have to master the file. Whatever happened in the next general election, there would therefore be someone who could brief the Government and make a recommendation.

I was fairly sure that legislation would not occur before the next Parliament. Even if it did, I would have to convince a minister that action should be taken or, better, had to be taken. I therefore decided to push the issue of breaches of national and international Treaty obligations. This would have several effects:

- it would increase the priority of my claim for legislative time, especially if I could show that the UK would lose money by way of damages if my proposal was not brought into law;
- the Civil Service would be bound to examine the issue more closely in line with its policy of avoiding embarrassment and loss;
- I might be able to argue that English law was superseded or overridden by European law and that the change I sought had, in effect, already happened. I did manage this, but in a peculiar way. I abolished the monopoly for non-UK citizens, not for UK ones, simply by interpretation of EU law;
- it would increase the chances of press coverage.

I decided to get Labour on my side before any election and hopefully to promise to bring in reform as and when they were elected. I also decided to contact the Liberal Democrats. Although they had no chance of a majority, their support could be helpful against either party. Liberal Democrats had a meritocratic outlook, basically against ancient privileges.

THE MEDIA

If you travel on public transport a lot, you get plenty of time to read the newspapers. You soon notice that the media favour certain themes at the expense of others. If, like me, you read practically any paper you find abandoned, you find that the same stories re-appear. A story on whatever subject which is printed by one of the qualities will very probably appear in the others after a lapse of time.

There are various explanations for this phenomenon. One is that journalists are pressed for time and competing for column space. The fact that a story has been seen as fit to print by *The Times* gives it a kind of seal of approval. Journalists from one newspaper read others and trade papers not normally read by the public for stories; in a word, for news.

In Appendix 5, I list books which have studied the media closely and some of which contain techniques and ideas for maximising press coverage.

My own knowledge was derived from newspaper articles and observation. I reasoned that key points the media liked to play up (insofar as they were relevant to my kind of issue) were:

- the struggle of the lone individual/eccentric against the establishment;
- the absurd and antiquated practices of the legal professions;
- the way in which English Governments and courts are being forced to change English law to conform to European law;
- the anomalies of the City of London and its medieval traditions.

What I needed to do was frame my story to fit media views of what a good story is. I would then get published and the issue would start to come into the public domain. I would be harder to ignore.

MY SPECIFIC CIVIL SERVICE DEPARTMENTS

In line with my aim of getting the buck to stop somewhere, I set out my short list of relevant government departments to contact. These were as follows.

The Office of Fair Trading (OFT)

This department was responsible, amongst other things, for supervising UK competition law. It seemed an ideal place to start if I wanted to get rid of a medieval monopoly. I soon confirmed my suspicion that UK competition law was highly formalistic and technical. The fact that a practice or monopoly might be completely uncompetitive in the eyes of the public cut no ice with the OFT. In particular, if a monopoly had been put in place by a statute (as the Scrivener monopoly had been), the OFT considered it had no power to do anything at all. Nonetheless, getting the OFT out of the way at the outset meant that I could not be directed to them by anyone else who wanted to get my file off their desk. Secondly, it was evident that the OFT could see that the monopoly was uncompetitive. My complaint to them meant a file was opened there and the OFT would then be able to give its view when consulted by the Government or other branches of the Civil Service.

The Lord Chancellor's Department (LCD)

This department gave legal advice to the Government and other branches of the Civil Service. It was large, but under-staffed, given the amount and variety of legal questions it was constantly called on to answer. It was also responsible for the supervision of the legal professions. However, the notarial profession was still under the control of the Archbishop of Canterbury and, hence, escaped the direct supervision of the LCD.

I felt that the last thing the LCD wanted was to have to take on more work, least of all take charge of another legal profession with an ancient medieval monopoly. It would be sanctioning the monopoly by not directing the profession to end it. I also thought that the many incidents in which the UK Government had failed to properly implement EU law would make the LCD wary of advice which could put the Government in further breach of EU Treaty obligations. These failures had led, in many cases, to successful claims for damages against the UK, because people affected had sued the Government for the resulting loss. A key example was the case of the Spanish fishermen.

THE SPANISH FISHERMEN AND *FRANCOVICH* DAMAGES

The Conservative Government had been concerned about over-fishing in UK waters. It had passed a law to make it obligatory that boats flying the British flag (and so allowed to fish in the area around the UK designated as the British fishing quota area) had to be 75% or more owned by British nationals. Boats already registered had to re-register. This meant that Spanish fishermen, amongst others, who had wished to fish in this area, were at a disadvantage. Previously, they had effectively bought the right to fish from British fishermen by setting up companies in the UK which owned boats. The boats flew the British flag, but the Spanish shareholders took the profits. The new law stopped them from doing so or, at least, discriminated against them. They sued to recoup the loss. Although the amount of damages had not yet been settled, it was clear they would win and that compensation would run into many millions.

The European law case (called *Francovich*) which established that they could win was in fact on an entirely different matter – that of pension rights for workers in Italy. It was clear in both cases that government failure to properly implement European law could lead to a direct liability for the Government if the individuals affected could show that their loss was directly caused by the Government's action or failure to act. Compensation for such losses came to be known as *Francovich* damages.

I thought that I could establish a potential *Francovich* damages claim and that this would motivate those considering my file to do so with some care, especially if I made sure to hammer home the point.

The European Commission

The European Commission was another overworked group of civil servants. The Commission advises the European Commissioners on all the matters for which they are responsible, for example, competition law, harmonisation of laws and taxes, enforcement against firms or States; indeed, all the administration of the EU. Yet the entire staff of the Commission amounts to less than the numbers employed by the BBC.

Furthermore, the Court which ultimately enforces European law, the European Court of Justice (ECJ), was itself very much clogged by cases. Even a cast iron instance of breach of European law usually took years to come to court. The Commission had to exercise a lot of discretion as to what breaches it would look at and how it would deal with them. Negotiation was always preferable to enforcement, unless there was no alternative.

More significantly, the ECJ had decided that Member States could discriminate against their own nationals. It was forbidden, however, to discriminate against nationals from other States. So, the French Government, for example, could not charge students coming to study in France from other EU countries any more than it charged its own students. There had to be a level playing field for all.

Logically, if the playing field is level, no discrimination is possible against anyone, be they a national of your own State or that of another EU State, but this is not what happens. Recently, Scottish universities decided to charge higher fees to English students than to Scottish ones. This is allowed under EU law, since, although English and Scottish students are from different counties, they are both from the same State, the UK. However, the Scottish universities could not have charged French, German or Italian students any more than they charged Scottish ones.

EU law textbooks see this as an anomaly. I suggest that the ECJ has simply decided to ignore the strict letter of EU law to reduce its workload. After all, the problem is almost always that countries discriminate against the outsider, the foreigner. The ECJ had, and still has, enough to do trying to stop abuses of the common kind, that is, treating foreigners more harshly than one's own nationals. Taking on the task of ironing out all discrimination was too much.

THE FUNDAMENTAL FREEDOMS AND ME

Under the Treaties that created the EU, the right to provide services and/or to establish oneself in a foreign Member State is fundamental. So is the rule against companies or groups of them engaging in anti-competitive behaviour.

Both principles had been defended and reaffirmed time and again by the ECJ. Member States had lost case after case when they had tried to prevent nationals of other Member States from supplying services on their soil or had made it more difficult for them to do so.

The principles were subject to various exceptions. In particular, the ECJ and the Commission tended to see a reason to intervene only when the behaviour or practice was likely to significantly affect or distort competition within the common market or a significant part of it. My problem was that I wanted to move from one part of a Member State, Greater London, to another part of the same State, the City of London and three miles around it. Since I was a UK national, I had no right of free movement that the EU Treaty would protect. The Commission would not take up my case.

I noted the absurdity, however. Had I been French and barred from working in the City of London, I would have been protected, since I was trying to exercise rights to move across borders. Being English, I had no rights at all.

I decided to twist the issue round. I reasoned that the monopoly must already be illegal under EU law, since it forbade entry to the City to work as a notary unless and until one had become a member of the Worshipful Company of Scriveners; illegal as against non-UK nationals, that is. I would find a way to demonstrate this, thus ending the absolute monopoly at a stroke.

I reasoned that if the Scriveners were operating a restriction on numbers (and the fact that there had only been around 30 Scrivener notaries at any one time for at least 100 years struck me as unlikely to be a coincidence), this too would be (in my view) illegal, as would be making joining their guild a precondition of practice. Likewise, requiring foreign notaries to serve five years' articles would also be struck down by EU law.

In short, the chief ways of controlling entry to the London market would all be illegal as against non-UK nationals. Further, by ending barriers against foreign notaries, the absurdity of such barriers would be highlighted. Not even the most fervent supporter of the EU could be in favour of a situation in which foreign notaries were better placed to compete in London than UK ones were. I thought that the monopoly was only held in place because the exclusion was total. There were very few Scriveners. That was the way it was and always would be.

Once it was admitted that anybody could practise in London, without five years' articles and without restriction on numbers, resentment would be felt, because the only people with these freedoms were not from the UK. I reasoned that many notaries were of a conservative bent and would start to demand equal treatment. This would split the united front I perceived in the attitudes of the Notaries' Society, the Faculty Office and the Scriveners. More people would become allied to my cause since, now, they had something to lose, the work Scriveners could lose to competitors. That work would now go to foreigners.

EUROPEAN COMPETITION LAW

I thought that the monopoly infringed European competition law, although not simply because it was a monopoly, however, since monopolies were permitted under EU law. When the EU was formed, most of the Member States had many State-run enterprises which were *de facto* monopolies, such as electricity companies or the post office. They were hardly likely to have signed up to a Treaty, under which they were in default immediately.

However, abuse of a monopoly position was against EU law, as was unfair exclusion of competitors. So, the ECJ had decided, was having the benefit of a monopoly, but not being in a position to serve all the customers who were in your area. My own view was that the Scrivener monopoly was in breach of all of these points. The trick was to convince the Commission that I was right.

Initial correspondence with the Commission showed a tendency on their part to want to rid themselves of the issue. I thought that this was part of the work reduction tendency evident throughout the EU. I decided not to push the issue with the EU. I would simply keep it as a back-up weapon in my relations with the British authorities. After all, phase two of my plan was to end all the notarial monopolies in Europe. I would then need the UK authorities on my side convincing the Commission to act.

UK ENFORCEMENT OF EUROPEAN LAW – COUNCIL DIRECTIVE (89/48/EEC)

The Commission had been seeking a means of easing cross-border movement for workers and the self-employed. Part of the problem had been that people in ostensibly the same profession in different countries had been given different training in each country. Training for butchers, bakers or dentists, for example, was different in each State. Nation States could justify excluding foreign workers on the grounds that they did not have the proper qualifications. While this was sometimes justified, at other times, it was the familiar tale of national chauvinism and disguised protectionism.

The first efforts to get around this had been by harmonising qualifications. Teams of experts from each country would meet and analyse the core knowledge needed to be an optician, carpenter or baker and devise a common curriculum. Once this was studied and passed, the student could qualify to practice in all the EU countries.

The problem was that this approach took forever. It was therefore decided to pass the General Directive on Mutual Recognition of Qualifications. Under this system, a student qualified in the usual way, then, if he or she wished to work abroad, sent details of subjects studied and experience gained to the State authorities in the country to which they wanted to move ('the host country'). It was the duty of any host country to examine the dossier sent and decide whether or not the training already received was adequate for practice in the host country. If it was, the migrant could set up in practice. If not, the migrant could be required either:

(a) to undergo a period of supervised practice in the host country to ensure that they could do the job according to local standards and expectations; or

(b) to pass extra examinations which concentrated only on the knowledge the migrant did not have which was essential to practice that profession in the host country.

The host country could require one or the other of these methods, but not both. The migrant could choose which method of adaptation suited him or her best.

The Directive was the 48th Directive passed in 1989, hence its short name of 89/48. It was very successful at unlocking many of the difficulties that had previously beset would be migrants. Previously, in the absence of an agreed core curriculum, migrants were faced with the prospect of having to start again from scratch and re-qualify in each country they moved to.

It seemed to me that this was the perfect tool for cracking the Scrivener monopoly. In the case of the legal professions, an exception had been made. Instead of the migrant being able to choose between a supervised period of practice and undergoing a test, it was the host State that would decide what would be undergone. In every case, they had decided to impose a test of knowledge. I thought that this is what the Scriveners and other notaries would choose. Supervising competitors is not good business and tends to give them too much of an insight into your business. I found out that each State was responsible for appointing an official who made sure that this Directive was implemented and that the Directive should have been fully carried out by 1991. I thought I would find out what had happened to the notaries under the Directive.

GENERAL POINTS

- I have spent some time analysing the players, since one needs to be aware of where they are in order to be ready for their next move.
- Normally, there are some key areas of pressure to which organisations are susceptible.
- Fear of loss is one of the key motives, I suggest, for people or organisations to behave as they do. With bureaucratic organisations, I would suggest this is by far the strongest motive of all. The loss can be of money, but is more often a fear of loss of face. Bad publicity, or the threat of it, is very powerful.

The same point can motivate many people in different ways. I was sure that the fact that foreign notaries would be able to work in London would inflame the 'little Englanders'. However, the absurdity of the monopoly would get the rest on my side. I could touch many people, without having to share the rest of their political baggage. I suggest that one needs to realise that people have their uses regardless of their political shade. One needs good arguments and this is what I now turned to providing.

CHAPTER 4

WINNING THE ARGUMENT

Those who cannot or will not disclose their arguments have none and know it.

The author.

There are two arguments to be won. The first is to persuade people you are right. The second is to persuade the Government to act as you wish.

The problem for the reformer is lack of numbers. The status quo often has plenty of people to defend it. Therefore, the case for change needs to be well thought out and take account of all defences. You need to know the enemy's case better than it does, so that you can summarise it and defeat it.

Apart from the intellectual argument, the authorities always have two basic arguments for leaving things the way they are:

(a) the first is that the present situation is the best that can reasonably be achieved;

(b) the second is that any change would require too much time or effort and would deflect time from other, more pressing issues.

According to the first argument, any change would probably be for the worse. The present situation has been arrived at by a consideration of all the relevant considerations and balancing them in the light of the public interest. Change could disturb that delicate balance. Of course, this is usually poppycock, but the argument needs to be dealt with. The most effective counter is twofold:

• showing that the present status quo is due to historical factors which are no longer relevant;

• demonstrating that the status quo will or must change in any event. This argument is strongest when one can show that the present situation contravenes government policy, international Treaty obligations or is absurd.

One needs to be careful with criticisms of the status quo. The whole established order tends to rally to its defence, since those who question it are implicitly arguing that those in power (or those advising them) have not done their job correctly.

As mentioned earlier, continuity in government policy is assured by the Civil Service and by consultation with those affected by policies, such as professional associations, lobby groups and others. To suggest that things need to change seems to criticise the recommendations that civil servants and others have made which have led to the current status quo. Often, these are the very people who need to be convinced, or neutralised, in order to win the argument. Blaming the need for change on a changed situation or international obligations helps to save face.

PRIORITIES

The second argument used to defend the status quo is that there is not enough time to deal with your issue. You may be right, but giving time to you would mean something else had to be left undone.

Of course, this argument is correct. Getting what you want will probably mean parliamentary time is needed and no government is guaranteed more than one term in office. The Government can always lose the next election. Putting in your amendment will inevitably push something else out.

I suggest that the best way of dealing with this is to downplay the amount of time that is needed. Many matters can be dealt with quickly. If what you need is repeal of legislation, this can be done alongside routine government legislative activity. Many old statutes are repealed or revised every year in uncontroversial Commons activity. Yours could be slotted in there by simply making the appropriate additional repeals in a Bill repealing other legislation.

If you need a law passed which will bring new rights or duties into effect, time will be needed. But there is no reason, again, why what you want cannot be tacked on to some planned government legislation. I experienced some resistance from civil servants to my plan to make proposed abolition of the Scrivener monopoly part of any forthcoming Bill on any subject, but there is no constitutional reason why it could not have been added to the end of a Bill on foxhunting (provided the Bill's long title had mentioned the subject – see Appendix 3 for technical details on the passing of Acts of Parliament). It is simply neater to put separate subjects in separate Bills.

The other way of raising your project in the priority list is by emphasising the benefits the Government will gain from adopting it and the loss and embarrassment it will suffer if it does not. Later in this chapter, I will give an example of this as it came up in my own campaign.

THE SILENT ENEMY

Often, those who benefit from the status quo prefer to say nothing about the reasons that justify things staying the way they are. That silence must be broken. It is a sign of the current strength of their position that it is unquestioned and no one thinks of asking for or providing justifications.

Yet, that silence is also weakness. It can hide a complete absence of justification. People have become so used to the way things are that they have no defence ready when they are forced to provide one. Victory for the reformer can be almost instantaneous – at least on the intellectual level – since the other side have become lazy in power or always were.

I hope that the Freedom of Information Bill will have teeth. At present, it can be very difficult to find out much about what either governments, the Civil Service or people on the other side of the debate from you think about an issue.

Civil Service rules currently require civil servants to keep documents and information confidential if it is explicitly or implicitly supplied to them in confidence. This can be a great hindrance and may remain as an obstacle in the future, depending on the final form of the Freedom of Information Act. That being the case, I suggest that it is vital to get inside the skin of your opponents. Learn to see the world as they do and you will both be able to predict their arguments and their next move in the game.

MAKING THE IMPLICIT EXPLICIT

One of the key points to remember is that getting people to spring to the defence of the status quo is a large part of the way to victory. Until the reasons for the status quo have been articulated, the current legal situation is not a position. It is simply the way things are. Since there is often no particular reason why things should be one way, rather than another, the mere expression of the reasons for a policy exposes it to attack, because better reasons can always be thought of for a new policy by those who are motivated.

MAKING A GREAT CASE

I decided to make every argument I could for retention of the monopoly and defeat it. This would hopefully have the effect of persuading people to my point of view straight away. If I had missed anything, I was sure my opponents would point it out.

The Law Society

Since time was short, I decided to kill two birds with one stone. I wrote to the Law Society asking them to take up my case. I argued that all solicitors were barred from acting in the monopoly area and it had a duty to act. I set out the arguments for the monopoly as follows:

(a) Scriveners were more qualified than solicitors for notarial work as practised in the City of London. They had different qualifications. They all studied at least two languages and acted as translators of legal documents;

(b) it would be dangerous to allow people to act as notaries without the training of a Scrivener notary;

(c) the monopoly did not exist, since clients could always go out of London for notarial services;

(d) the monopoly had been there so long, it would be wrong to take it away.

My counter-arguments were (using the same numbering):

(a) although Scriveners did study different exams to solicitors, the differences were not relevant to practise as a notary. Proof of this was that solicitors could be notaries anywhere in England and Wales (even in South Kensington) without studying the Scrivener curriculum. If the subjects were necessary to be a notary, you would need them everywhere. In particular, the fact that Scrivener notaries studied legal translation was not essential for the job or the protection of the public. If it was, the Master of the Faculties would have compelled all notaries to qualify as translators;

(b) clients would be protected from people doing work they were not qualified to do by the usual professional rule that a solicitor or notary should not do work they are not competent to do. If there was concern about competence, additional exams could be set. Strangely, this was not being recommended. However, one would still have to deal with the question why higher standards were needed only in the area covered by the Scrivener monopoly. If the concern was protection of the public, surely the monopoly should be extended to the rest of the country or, at least, to the major cities. Solicitors, once qualified, could set up in the City without any problem at all. Why should a different rule apply to notaries?;

(c) this argument missed the point. Either the public needed the protection of the Scrivener monopoly or it did not. Indeed, since the monopoly was geographical, at the perimeter of the monopoly area, the public was already ably served by non-Scrivener notaries. The act of a notary was the act of a notary and was recognised everywhere in the world, whether or not it was the act of a Scrivener notary. Surely, that was all that mattered? If the acts of a non-Scrivener notary were less effective than that of Scrivener, surely some health warning should be attached to them to protect the consumer or notaries outside London should be prevented from doing some notarial acts? In any event, the monopoly could be retained, but reduced to an area within a symbolic 100 yards of Mansion House. Tradition would be served and competition introduced at the same time;

(d) I did not know for a fact that this argument would be used, but thought it was what I would think if I were a Scrivener. I argued that competition is simply a fact of life and good for the consumer. No one was proposing that Scriveners should be abolished, simply that competition should be allowed. In nearly every case where people had argued that introducing competition would be a disaster, the feared cataclysm had not happened. Solicitors knew this for a certainty, since the end of the conveyancing monopoly had not meant the end of the solicitors' profession.

I did not realise until later that this initial letter contained all the arguments that (to my knowledge) were ever used.

ACTION BY THE LAW SOCIETY

The above letter went off to the Law Society on 31 July 1995. It had been typed by my thumbs on a Psion Organiser, Series 3a. I found that the organiser saved a phenomenal amount of time. I was able to keep up with my job and the campaign simply by using otherwise idle moments on the London public transport system to type my campaign letters. But I digress.

The Law Society sent my letter to the two local Law Societies it considered relevant, representing solicitors in the City of London and the City of Westminster respectively. Neither Society was enthusiastic about abolition, although nobody could see any reason why the monopoly should continue. The Scriveners were also asked for their comments and I read their eventual reply with interest.

THE SCRIVENER REPLY

This arrived in January 1996. It made the following points:

- if there was competition in the monopoly area, the Scrivener notaries would wither away. They needed the monopoly to guarantee them enough work to practise full time as notaries;
- solicitor notaries were less skilled than Scrivener notaries. In particular, the Scriveners had foreign language skills, tried and tested by examination. They had also studied some 'foreign law'.

Proof was lacking of either point and I sent the Law Society a detailed letter, examining the qualifications of Scriveners. I noted from the Scriveners' own examination rules that the examinations to become a Scrivener notary were largely set and marked by other Scrivener notaries. The standard aspired to was that of a second class external degree from the University of London. This included lower second class, I observed, and, hence, a mark of 50% would be enough.

Since solicitor trainees in the City of London would normally be expected to have an upper second class degree, marked by external examiners, this fact alone was enough to put a question mark beside the 'superior' standards of the Scriveners. I had qualified as a translator myself via the Institute of Linguists. Their own view was that, to be a translator, you needed to have both a degree and a postgraduate qualification in the language you were going to translate from. Further, you should only translate into your native language, since this was usually the only one in which you understood all the nuances. After the academic stage of training, you needed practice.

I thought that the Scrivener qualifications clearly did not meet this standard, since a postgraduate degree was not required. Further, Scriveners translated into foreign languages, not just into their native language. I made this clear to the Law Society. In any event, the language qualifications were irrelevant, since all other notaries were practising without them being required.

Close inspection of the languages actually studied by Scriveners showed that they were basically all modern European languages. What if the document was in Swahili, Chinese or Hindi? I reasoned that the Scriveners must use hired translators. I visited some of their offices and collected their brochures. It was obvious that some Scriveners were offering to arrange translations into languages which they had not studied. If they could use translators, so could anyone. Detailed examination of the 'foreign law' studied by Scriveners showed, in my view, that this knowledge was not required to be deep. It too was irrelevant, since other notaries were practising without it.

Admissions by the Scriveners

An interesting aspect of the Scrivener reply was that it defined the job of a notary. I noted that it clearly defined this as being things all notaries did, that is, drawing up and witnessing legal documents. The translations and foreign law advice were separate. I thought this was an accurate statement. Coming from the Scriveners themselves, it was priceless for other aspects of my campaign, notably with regard to English recognition of foreign notaries.

In short, my argument would be that translating and giving advice on foreign law was no part of the essential job of a notary. Such skills could not therefore be required of migrant notaries. But, no doubt, the Scriveners would still require them of English notaries. The unfairness of this would be apparent to anyone who thought about it.

GETTING THE LAW SOCIETY TO ACT

Although the Law Society agreed with me that there was no justification for the monopoly, it refused to act. I pursued the matter through its various committees, but to no avail. The matter was 'not a sufficiently high priority'.

I decided to make it one. I appealed to the then President, Martin Mears, and to the candidates in the campaign to be the next President of the Law Society. None, save Anthony Bogan, a solicitor running on a radical reform ticket, could manage to take a definite position on the issue. I began to understand why the Law Society kept losing campaigns. Nobody dared take a stand on anything. It was a culture of committees. 'If in doubt, set up a further sub-committee and pass a resolution to discuss it later' seemed to be the motto. The Law Society was often in doubt.

Having exhausted all reasonable channels, I opted for the brute force option. Under the constitution of the Law Society, a resolution signed by 100 or more members could oblige the Law Society to call a meeting to debate it. That meeting could either approve the resolution or submit it to the whole membership by a postal ballot. It was a very expensive process. I drafted a resolution to the effect that the Law Society was instructed by its members to push for the end of the monopoly. I sent it in just after the Law Society old guard had won another postal ballot called for by reformers.

I chose my time carefully. I reasoned that the last thing the Law Society wanted was another public battle. In my case, the battle would be about why they could not write a letter on behalf of solicitors asking for a barrier to work to be removed. Since many solicitors were still angry with the Law Society for failing to defend the conveyancing monopoly, I thought it unlikely that solicitors would support the Scriveners keeping theirs. The Society would lose face if the ballot went ahead. The only way to stop it was to give me what I wanted. So they did. The Law Society voted to make ending the Scrivener monopoly its official policy.

The Law Society decided to write to the Lord Chancellor to ask for the abolition of the monopoly. I knew that their support was reluctant, but the letter was sent. Formally, I had them on my side. That was all that would be necessary.

GENERAL POINTS

- The research undertaken about the players proved its worth in framing the arguments. The other side had no arguments I had not already countered.

- The failure of the Law Society to support me initially was a blow, but strengthened my resolve. Since they had no intellectual arguments against my case, all they could do was talk about 'priorities'. Since all they finally did was write a one page letter, that was obviously a code for something else. In my view, the Law Society was still stuck in a time warp. It was living in a world of gentlemen whose motto was 'Don't attack my monopoly and I won't attack yours'. Since solicitors had now lost their monopolies, this attitude was hopelessly out of date.

- Popularity is unnecessary; the result is the only thing that counts. I would not be liked at the Law Society, but I would be respected. More importantly, I had their vote when the final head count of those for and against the monopoly was made.

Mentally, I could now see victory. I wanted to break the monopoly via the European route, then push for abolition for UK nationals after the election expected in 1997. I will deal with this in the next chapter.

CHAPTER 5

SIDESTEPPING VIA EUROPE

There can be no whitewash at the White House.

Richard Nixon.

For me, one of the most exciting moments in the fall of the Communist dictatorships in Eastern Europe was the downfall of President Ceauçescu of Romania. Expert political commentators had been sure that, even though other Communist regimes had fallen, Romania would resist. The people had been too repressed for opposition to develop. In the end, Romania collapsed the quickest. Someone booed Ceauçescu at a public rally. The crowd took up the cry. Ceauçescu visibly flinched and had lost control. He lost power shortly after that. The power of the status quo is brittle everywhere. Even a small crack can bring the edifice down.

I sensed that the Scrivener monopoly was the same. Any gap in it would be fatal. It would undermine complete control. Therefore, if I could establish the right of foreigners to practise in the City of London without serving a five year apprenticeship or studying to be translators, the two biggest barriers to entry to the notarial profession in London would be removed. It would only be a matter of time and further pressure before the monopoly was ended for UK notaries.

I had a three stage plan:

(a) get the monopoly ended for foreigners;

(b) deal with the aftermath (which, I thought, would be an attempt to raise notarial qualifications);

(c) push for the end of the monopoly under the new Government.

The first job was to end the monopoly for foreign notaries, and for this I used Directive 89/48.

DIRECTIVE 89/48 – WHAT HAD HAPPENED?

The reader will recall that other EU notaries should already have been able to practise in London under the provisions for mutual recognition of qualifications. However, to every legal rule, there is usually an exception. In the case of the right for a professional to move freely across borders, there was the exception set out in Art 45 (previously Art 55) of the EU Treaty. This provided that the right of free movement did not apply to those activities which were connected with the exercise of 'official authority'.

When I contacted the Department of Trade and Industry (DTI) civil servant dealing with making sure that the UK had complied with Directive 89/48, I found that the Notaries' Society, the Worshipful Company of Scriveners and the Faculty Office had each filed separate submissions to the DTI, claiming that the notarial profession was protected by this provision. I never managed to see the actual submissions that any of these bodies had made. This was due to civil service rules on the confidentiality of submissions. It was a handicap in making a good counter-argument but, luckily, one I could overcome. I had to convince the DTI and their legal advisers that the notarial profession did not exercise official authority.

THE MEANING OF 'OFFICIAL AUTHORITY'

The trouble was that the Treaty had not defined what was meant by 'official authority'. The meaning had to be worked out by examining the legal cases on the subject and thinking about the general principles of EU law.

The need to coerce

The chief case on the meaning of 'official authority' had involved a Dutch lawyer, a Mr Reyners, who had been refused permission to practise in Belgium (*Reyners v Belgium* No 2/74 [1974] ECR 631). The ECJ decided that official authority meant that you had to be exercising powers of coercion over citizens, powers outside the general law. That definition had been quoted with approval in subsequent ECJ cases. The court decided that the legal work in question (giving advice, appearing in court) simply did not fit the definition. Mr Reyners could practise in Belgium.

My first stop, then, was to check what, if any, things that an English notary did involved such coercive power. The short answer was none. I was puzzled that the notarial groups had even attempted to run this argument. The essence of 95% of all notarial work in England was that a client would come to you with a document already prepared. You, as a notary, had to certify or record that you had seen the person sign the document in your presence and that you had evidence of their identity. There seemed to be absolutely nothing in this relationship between notary and client which involved the slightest amount of power, let alone the notary coercing the client to do something.

THE *ACTE AUTHENTIQUE*

It seemed to me that the only type of notarial act which could involve power was the type known in France as an *acte authentique*. Two or more people could come to see a notary and sign a contract before him or her. Such a contract was known as *an acte authentique* and could, in some circumstances, be enforced against a party to it who had failed to meet their end of the bargain, without the need to go to court to prove the terms of the contract. The fact that the contract was made in solemn form, as an *acte authentique*, before a notary, made the contract difficult to break and easy to enforce. This was held up by continental notaries as an example of the 'official authority' notaries exerted. However, there were at least three problems with this reasoning:

(a) the *acte authentique* was not the act of the notary, but of the people who came to see the notary. The notary was really a scribe, as she or he had been in Roman times, faithfully recording the intentions of the parties. In order to exert official authority, the notary would have had to have been able to compel the parties to come into his or her office and sign something they did not wish to sign. This was not the case;

(b) in England, the clear position was that notarial acts were never enforceable in themselves. If a contract was contained in a notarised document, or drawn up by a notary and signed in his or her presence, the English courts took no more notice of it than any other contract drawn up by a lawyer or a layperson. Indeed, *Brooke's Notary* actually stated that English notaries did not even seek the power to have their acts recognised as judgements;[1]

(c) the idea behind the official authority exception was that, in certain circumstances, you could refuse to accept non-nationals. In *Brooke's Notary*, however, I found that there was no nationality requirement to be an English notary.[2] Since there was no objection on the grounds of nationality, there could be no defence on the grounds of official authority.

Therefore, even if French notaries could claim official authority, English ones could not, since they themselves had admitted they did not have it. English notaries were not even seeking 'official authority' and this was admitted in *Brooke's Notary*.

PROPORTIONALITY

My next argument was that even if English notaries did exercise official authority, they still could not exclude foreigners. I read all the relevant law

---

1 *Brooke's Notary* 1992, Sweet & Maxwell, p 73.

2 *Ibid*, p 44.

cases and found that the defence of official authority had *never* succeeded. The reason for this was clearly stated in the decisions of the ECJ. If the exception was granted easily and nation States could ban foreign nationals from migrating, then it would drive a coach and horses through the free movement provisions of the EU Treaty.

Even better, the ECJ had decided that even where it could be demonstrated that someone exercised official authority, this did not automatically mean that foreigners could be excluded. The response had to be proportional to the problem. To quote another ECJ decision (*R v Minister for Agriculture, Fisheries and Food ex p Fedesa*, Case C-331/88):

> The Court has consistently held that the principle of proportionality is one of the general principles of Community law. By virtue of that principle, the lawfulness of the prohibition of an economic activity is subject to the condition that the prohibitory measures are appropriate and necessary in order to achieve the objectives legitimately pursued by the legislation in question; when there is a choice between several appropriate measures, recourse must be had to the least onerous and the disadvantages caused must not be disproportionate to the aims pursued.

In short, even if the notaries could establish that they exercised official authority, they would need to prove its relevance.

In other words, what was the objective behind the use of the official authority defence? What problem was there which could only be solved by banning foreigners from migrating to your country? I never did find out the specific reasons the Notaries' Society, the Scriveners and the Faculty Office had, although I made sure to ask.

It seemed that there were two possible reasons for blocking the right of other EU nationals to come here:

(a) that the profession exercised official authority, and so foreign notaries had no rights to come to the UK anyway;

(b) that they would not be competent to do the job.

It seemed impossible to prove that official authority was being exercised by English notaries. It was hard to suggest that they had much authority at all. So, the only defence was on the basis of competence, and this was exactly what Directive 89/48 was designed to ensure. It was entirely proper to set an aptitude test for EU notaries wishing to practise as English ones. It was not acceptable simply to exclude migrants altogether. But not complying with Directive 89/48 would amount to exclusion since, otherwise, EU notaries would have to re-qualify as English ones by starting again from scratch. Crucially, if they wanted to work in the Scrivener monopoly area, they would have to serve five years' articles' to an existing Scrivener notary.

FREE MOVEMENT TO WHERE?

The heart of my argument was that Directive 89/48 meant that EU notaries could move directly into London without needing five years' articles and without needing any special translation examinations or foreign law examinations. They could only be made to study the knowledge essential to being a notary. That was the same for all notaries, inside London or outside it. London could not be a special case, excluded from the right to free movement. I was concerned to quash the argument that, since English notaries could not practise in London unless they became Scriveners, neither could EU notaries.

To me, the argument was simple. A right to practise in another country must mean a right to practise in all of that country, not just most of it. Around 15 million people worked or lived in or around London. That was more than the entire population of several EU States. London on its own therefore represented a substantial part of the EU. Access to it could not be denied.

An obligation to act

I therefore pressed the DTI to oblige the notarial profession to comply with Directive 89/48. I argued that non-compliance would lead to a potential liability for *Francovich* damages to EU notaries who were prevented from working in London.

PUSHING THE FILE

The DTI could not act without legal advice. It sought this from the Lord Chancellor's Department (LCD). Was the notarial profession liable to comply with Directive 89/48 or not?

The response took a very long time. I decided to lodge an official complaint. I am glad that I did. The notary file finally moved on to the desk of someone capable of reaching a decision.

I prepared a detailed submission to the LCD, arguing that the official authority defence was not applicable and, if it was, could not lead to excluding non-nationals since, first, non-nationals were already allowed to work here and, secondly, the existence of an aptitude test would mean that all migrant notaries would have to prove their competence. I won the argument and notaries were directed to comply with Directive 89/48. Further, it was agreed that EU notaries would be able to work in London, including the monopoly area, without serving articles.

THE AFTERMATH

I thought that, when I won the right for foreign notaries to practise in London, the Scriveners would only have two lines of defence:

(a) the first would be to claim that they were a separate profession and could set special exams, still imposing a requirement that one be a translator and study 'foreign law';

(b) the second would be to upgrade the examination requirements to qualify as a Scrivener notary. This requirement would be imposed on all new UK notaries. Harder exams could then be justified for foreign notaries.

Of course, it is impossible to know the mind of even one person, let alone a group. I would not say that the Scrivener response was calculated in the way I describe. Most of the time, I suggest, our real motives are not even known to ourselves. I was sure that, if the Scriveners reacted as I thought, they would be thinking to themselves that they did what they did in the public interest, not their own. The only relevant criterion would be the maintenance of standards. These needed to be upgraded in the light of changed circumstances.

The result would, however, be the same, qualification inflation. Competitors would be excluded, but not by conscious design.

NEW QUALIFICATIONS FOR NOTARIES

It was in February 1997 that the LCD made the decision that Directive 89/48 must be complied with, but there was no immediate compliance by either Scriveners or the Faculty Office.

I had a dull period waiting for the May 1997 election to take place and the new Labour Government to get its early Bills out of the way. I knew that the Government intended to reform the administration of the courts and the legal professions, and decided to wait to see what their timetable was. I then started to hear rumours that there was planned to be an increase in the qualifications required of notaries.

At this time, although examinations were required, it was still possible to be a solicitor, a general notary or a Scrivener without having a degree. Scriveners only needed O and A levels and then the examinations set by the Scriveners Company (which they considered equivalent to a degree).

It was now proposed that all notaries have a degree and undergo a course in notarial education. Exemptions would be possible from some subjects in the curriculum if one could show that one had previously studied them. Scriveners would also study this initial curriculum, but then would have to study a Masters degree in specialised subjects dealing with international law, and take articles or be supervised by a Scrivener for a further two years. There was no indication of what these subjects would be or that any university could be bothered to set up such a Masters. Nor was there any guarantee that there would be any articles available. The rules did, however admit that EU notaries could work in London.

Objections to the new rules

The new rules brought immediate opposition from some members of the ASN, who were solicitor notaries practising around London. The following points were made:

- the Scrivener education rules were excessive. A Masters degree was demanded in subjects which were not specified;
- articles would still be necessary and probably only very rarely available;
- there seemed to be an assumption that Scriveners were better since, to get to be one, you would need more qualifications than you would to be a notary outside the monopoly area;
- Scriveners already qualified would not have to re-qualify, but notaries qualified to practise outside London would have to sit the additional examinations and find and serve an apprenticeship to a Scrivener. Even after doing all that, it appeared that the Scriveners Company could still refuse to admit you;
- many of the proposed subjects, such as Roman law, bore no relevance to practice as a notary;
- the education requirements for notaries had been looked at in 1990. Nothing had happened since which required further increases in the time spent studying to become a notary.

I had predicted the educational rule changes to the DTI. I knew that the need to comply with Directive 89/48 would focus the mind of those running the profession on the essence of what it was to become a notary. In fact, not many exams were necessary. You could qualify as a notary under the 1990 rules simply by taking exams in land law and conveyancing, trusts and probate, notarial practice and bills of exchange. It was possible to become a notary without having a degree or being a member of any other legal profession at all. This meant that legal secretaries could qualify, as could licensed conveyancers or legal executives. They could also do so quite cheaply, since the exams were prepared for by private study, not by attendance at any college or institution.

Exclusion of the legal executives and licensed conveyancers

The proposed new rules effectively restricted entry to the profession to solicitors and barristers. The requirement to have a first degree stopped the majority of legal secretaries, legal executives and licensed conveyancers from qualifying since, usually, they had not taken degrees.

My own objections were similar to those of the ASN, but included the fact that the new rules still failed to comply with Directive 89/48. This is because two tests were proposed for migrant notaries. Passing the general notary test would allow them to practise in England and Wales, but not in the monopoly area. Passing the Scrivener test would enable them to practise everywhere in England and Wales, including the monopoly area.

The problem with this was that the Directive was quite clear; only one test was permitted. The notarial profession was suggesting two. Further, I argued that the migrant must know what the nature of the test is. It must be clear what he or she is to be examined on. There was no hint of this in either proposed test. The notarial authorities would simply look at each individual application, as it came along and decide what subjects had to be studied them.

Although it was certainly true that one had to take account of the specific knowledge of each applicant, this did not, to my mind, preclude setting out what the necessary knowledge was.

I thought that the real problem was that, when you actually looked at the essential knowledge needed to be a notary, you would come out with the same list of subjects for Scrivener and general notaries. If you went ahead and published this, people would realise that the intellectual justification for separating Scrivener notaries from others did not exist.

The result of the consultation period

The Faculty Office had invited comments from the profession, but it refused to get involved with the Scriveners new rules. These were matters for the Scriveners.

The rules were adopted for general notaries. The LCD refused to get drawn into the debate on the rules, arguing that the profession was under the supervision of the Master of the Faculties. The Scriveners did not finalise their Rules until six days after the First Reading of the Access to Justice Bill in December 1999. That Bill made no mention of notaries. The Scriveners then finally approved their rules. The fact that they did so at this point is, no doubt, pure coincidence.

New allies

Some of the notaries in the ASN had now had enough. Attempts to get the Scriveners to relax the monopoly had failed. The new rules would make it harder than ever to qualify as a Scrivener notary. They decided to act to end the monopoly.

ADMISSIONS BY THE FACULTY OFFICE

The Faculty Office decided to publish the results of the consultation period on its new website. It set the new rules and summarised arguments which had been sent in by notaries. The key point was at the end. Various notaries had complained about the complexity of the examinations and the number of subjects to be studied in the new general notary curriculum, and queried whether they were necessary in the real world of notarial work. But, the Faculty Office replied:

> The notarial profession is undivided in the sense that any notary, Scrivener or not, is authorised to perform any notarial act. The Scriveners have a geographical, not a qualitative jurisdiction. The Faculty Office doubts whether it has the power to create a profession divided between fully and partly qualified notaries able to perform different acts. Policing such a system would be difficult and expensive. Moreover, the reason for many notarial acts is so they may be recognised abroad. Those abroad should be able to rely on England and Wales notarial acts without having to enquire whether the particular act was one which the notary in question was entitled to perform.

As I mentioned when quoting this to the DTI, it is hard to think of a more definitive statement that there is only one notarial profession.

GENERAL POINTS

- I was defeated on my objections to the new Scrivener qualifications, but the Faculty Office statement more than made up for that. It officially confirmed what I and others had always argued – that the Scrivener monopoly was only a geographical one. It therefore had no reason to survive.
- The furore over the new rules pushed key people onto the side of abolition. I was no longer alone.
- The next step was to ask for abolition. This is the subject of the next chapter.

CHAPTER 6

ASKING FOR ABOLITION

Whatever you can, or dream you can, begin it. Boldness has genius, power and magic in it.

Goethe.

The only way to get a Bill passed is to ask for it to be passed. The indirect route to abolition had run its course. The struggle now had to move to Parliament. The credit for doing this goes to three key members of the ASN: Allen Labor; Hans Hartwig; and Tom Barker. They decided to try to get an amendment moved to the Competition Bill which would abolish the Scrivener monopoly. The method was simple, but effective:

(a) contact MPs who:

- might be sympathetic; or
- were from London constituencies;
- were directly involved in the scrutiny of the Competition Bill; and

(b) inform them of the existence of the Scrivener monopoly; and

(c) convince them it should be abolished; and

(d) ask them to move an amendment to the Competition Bill to abolish it.

It is impossible to do justice to the importance of taking this step. Although the move was not successful in the short term (since the Government did not adopt the amendment), it did set up abolition in the medium term. It gave us all valuable practice at direct lobbying.

THE COMPETITION BILL

Like many Bills that are passed by Parliament, this Bill had originated under a previous administration. It was intended to simplify existing competition law and to provide protection to people who might suffer from anti-competitive practices. It was a Bill promoted by the Department of Trade and Industry (DTI). This would have a large impact on the outcome of the lobbying process. In a nutshell, the argument used against the amendment to abolish the monopoly was that it was not 'within the scope of the Bill'. This means that when a Bill is first laid before Parliament, it has to have a description within it of what it will do (its 'scope'). So, a Bill to denationalise the railways will state that this is its object. Some Bills do a multitude of things. An Administration of Justice Bill, for example, will often contain clauses repealing old legislation in whole or in part and substituting new clauses in old legislation. It may also increase the penalties payable for offences. There are scales of fines, which can be charged for infractions of the law and these are periodically updated. It may also set out new rules for the administration of the estates of the deceased. However, all these matters will be mentioned in the Bill when it is first published (and are, therefore, matters which are 'within the scope of the Bill') and are thus matters which can be debated in the House and eventually become law.

Yet, amendments are often necessary to Bills since, for example:

- the Government realises it will run into too much opposition if it proceeds with the Bill as originally planned;

- the Government or the Civil Service decides it has made a mistake in drafting some parts of the Bill;

- the Government decides to accept amendments tendered by the opposition or its own supporters.

Amendments can be moved in either House of Parliament. Here, the bulk of amendments were moved at Committee stage. This is when the Bill is examined, clause by clause, by a group of MPs who are delegated the task. However, the MPs in a committee reflect the number of MPs each party has in the House. Government support is therefore highly important. It is also necessary not to antagonise the department and minister responsible for the Bill.

The problem with the Competition Bill is that it needed to have a lot of exceptions. A law which simply banned anti-competitive practices would have made the Post Office letter monopoly, the BBC licence fee and British Telecom's standing charges illegal at a stroke. All monopolies would have been banned. So, the DTI had been careful to exempt a large number of matters from the scope of the Bill. This included statutory monopolies like the Scrivener monopoly. The DTI was not keen to see this principle overturned.

LOBBYING THE COMMITTEE

Both the ASN and I separately lobbied to have an amendment made to the Bill to have the Scrivener monopoly removed. The ASN produced an interesting submission, which cleverly contrasted the London of 1801 (the year the statutory monopoly was granted) with London today. It drew attention to the following points:

- the geographical area covered by the monopoly was large and it was huge in terms of population and market. Yet, it had only 30 notaries. The public did not have enough choice and getting to see a notary could be difficult;

- many notaries who were not Scriveners had skills at least equal to those of Scriveners, but were not allowed to serve the public;
- although Scriveners had a monopoly which covered the City and a circle three miles around it, they nearly all worked in the City itself. This meant that millions of people were nowhere near a notary;
- the idea of a monopoly was antiquated and incompatible with today's society.

The points I made were similar. On reflection, however, I consider now that both submissions were far too long. My submission was over 10 pages long and the ASN's letter about the same. Both of us had made the mistake of assuming that other people would be as interested in the issue as we were. In fear of not making a comprehensive argument, we went on rather too long.

However, making a start got the ASN and, particularly, Allen Labor and myself, into the swing of contacting MPs. This was a new experience for all of us. Prior to this, I and others had simply asked our own constituency MPs to forward letters on our behalf. We were now starting to lobby people we had no connection with. Allen Labor managed to persuade several Liberal Democrat MPs to support abolition. I had the support of my own MP, Diane Abbott, and Austin Mitchell. Both the Liberal Democrats and Austin Mitchell tabled amendments to abolish the monopoly.

CONSULTATION ON ABOLITION

The key impact of lobbying MPs was that they started to bring the matter up with the LCD. The LCD decided to review the monopoly on behalf of the Government and wrote to all interested parties for their comments. Those consulted included not only the Master of the Faculties and the Scriveners, but also the ASN, the Law Society, the Bar and the Legal Executives. Unknown to us at the time, the Office of Fair Trading was also consulted.

Consultation was announced in a letter from the LCD, dated 29 May 1998. It referred to pressure on the Government to abolish the monopoly from 'several quarters' and specifically to the amendment to the Competition Bill tabled by the Liberal Democrat MP, David Chidgey. More strikingly, it went on to say that the Government was basically hostile to commercial monopolies and the position of the Scrivener monopoly was 'anomalous'. The Lord Chancellor was aware of concerns that, 'in a large area of central London, ordinary notarial services are effectively unavailable to any members of the public who might need them'. In short, the Government was considering abolition in the Competition Bill and wanted comments by the end of June.

Failure with the Competition Bill

Although comments were made and submitted by this deadline, the amendments tabled were not called for discussion and the Government did not move one itself to abolish the monopoly. The Competition Bill passed into law with the Scrivener monopoly intact.

It is hard to know what went wrong. I think the DTI resented having something tacked on to one of its Bills which it had not planned for. Legislative time for a DTI Bill should not be wasted on other departments' problems. The DTI wanted to leave monopolies alone in any event, let alone legal ones which could be tackled in the forthcoming Bill on the legal professions.

THE SUCCESS IN FAILURE

The essential point was that the Government had now consulted on abolition. All the arguments had been deployed. We did not know what the other side had said, but it did not take a genius to guess.

The Government had said it was against monopolies. It had perhaps been foreseeable that the DTI would object to this amendment, but there could be no such argument in respect of the Lord Chancellor's proposed Bill to reform the legal professions and the administration of justice. That was due in the next session and we hoped that, by then, the result of consultation on abolition would be known and the Government would adopt abolition as official policy. We had every reason to be optimistic. The reader will see in the next chapter how wrong we were.

CHAPTER 7

VICTORY AFTER DEFEAT

Parliament shut for summer recess in July 1998. The result of the consultation on abolition did not make its appearance. I and the ASN chased the civil servants responsible, but simply got the bland 'the Government is considering its advice and will decide in good time' type of letter one gets when the Government has decided not to make up its mind. We began to get nervous. Finally, I heard from a key civil servant that two decisions had been made:

(a) the Government would not be announcing the result of its consultation on abolition;

(b) the Government would, as, when and if it made a decision on abolition, be making one only in principle. The matter was too small to be a priority and would not figure in the Bill to reform the legal professions, which would be known as the Access to Justice Bill.

So it proved. The Access to Justice Bill was given its First Reading in Parliament on 2 December 1998. It contained proposals to reform the legal professions and, specifically, plans to make it easier for solicitors to qualify to appear as advocates in the highest courts and as judges. However, there was no mention of the notarial profession at all, let alone abolition of the monopoly. The Scriveners Company adopted their new rules on qualification on 8 December 1998. They would take effect on 1 February 1999.

We were defeated. Not only was the monopoly going to remain, but it would be harder to become a Scrivener than ever. As mentioned earlier, the Government would not be revisiting the legal professions again before the next election and probably not afterwards.

At least, we seemed to be defeated. Key members of the ASN and I decided to meet on 7 December 1998. We knew what would be in the Bill from the White Paper that the Government had published. The question was what could we do and why had we failed?

OUR ANALYSIS

The most likely reason, we considered, was that senior civil servants had decided to ease the passage of the Bill by ruthlessly cutting out anything that did not have to be in it. The more conspiratorial amongst us thought that the higher echelons of the Civil Service might actually support the monopoly. Yet, we agreed that abolition fitted in with the Government's professed agenda quite nicely. The White Paper which preceded the Bill had been at pains to stress the fact that the Government wanted to get rid of self-serving, antiquated legal practices which protected lawyers' own interests and fees. A monopoly the Government had said it was basically opposed to seemed ripe for abolition.

We doubted whether the Lord Chancellor even knew of our plan to abolish the monopoly. My own view was that our success so far was due to pressure. As lawyers with many clients, we all knew that the client who often got served quickest was the difficult one. You simply wanted to deal with his or her file quickly to cut the pain down of having to deal with their many phone calls. I argued that our seeming defeat was our strength, since the enemy would now be off their guard. I suggested that:

- we needed to increase the pain factor for the Civil Service and the Government. If it was easy to ignore us, they would;
- letters from MPs had been the key to getting consultation to abolish. Three times that number of letters would finish the job;
- the closed nature of Scrivener recruitment was likely to mean indirect sex and race discrimination (of course, this would be entirely unintentional). Support could be gained from organisations fighting for equal rights for these sections of society;
- the Government had shown that it was afraid of being embarrassed. The absurdity of the monopoly was apparent to anyone. The Access to Justice Bill was supposed to help the consumers of legal services and if our amendment was rejected, then the Bill would not be doing what it was supposed to do. Those who were arguing that the Bill was simply there to cut costs would gain additional force for their point of view;
- we had to widen the target and get anyone and everyone we could to write to the Lord Chancellor to urge the end of the monopoly. Family, friends, solicitors, notaries, clients, people we met at parties, every letter counted in increasing the pain factor and the workload for the Lord Chancellor's Department (LCD);
- we needed to get through to the Lord Chancellor direct. Obviously, his mail was screened. I therefore suggested we contact the close friend he had employed as a public relations person after the fiasco with regard to the refurbishment of his offices at the House of Lords. That person was Garry Hart, a City solicitor. The expense of redecoration had been huge and the publicity had largely been adverse. If we could suggest to Garry Hart that the Lord Chancellor had the makings of a large success or failure with regard to the issue of the monopoly, we might prevail on him to bring up the matter with the Lord Chancellor direct and thus bypass the Lord Chancellor's civil servants. I had found the telephone number of

Garry Hart at his office at the LCD and gave this to Tom Barker, who promised to ring him;

- I also suggested that our back-up weapon should be a threat to appear at the Lord Chancellor's public meetings in medieval costume, dressed in the style of a notary of the epoch. The reasoning was that this would certainly draw the attention of the press and seriously embarrass the Lord Chancellor;

- I intended, dressed as described, to deliver to the Lord Chancellor a petition I had already sent by letter to his Department. This was an appeal under s 11 of the Ecclesiastical Licences Act 1533. This Act provided that, when a faculty to practise as a notary had been unjustly refused by the Archbishop of Canterbury, one could appeal direct to the Lord Chancellor. It had subsequently been decided by the courts that this type of appeal should be directed through the courts. I decided that, since nothing is ever final in English law, I would ignore this decision and make my appeal direct. I planned to have it set out on parchment type paper and ask the Lord Chancellor to decide the case personally, as indeed he would have done in 1533. Since the present Lord Chancellor had described himself as comparable to Cardinal Wolsey, the Lord Chancellor of that time, I thought this was quite appropriate;

- I would threaten to sue the UK Government for breaches of the EU Treaty which were entailed by the continued existence of the Scrivener monopoly.

OUR PLAN OF CAMPAIGN

I volunteered to write to all MPs and to any relevant Lords for support for an amendment to abolish the monopoly, which I would attach to my letters. I thought Austin Mitchell would support us again and table a new amendment to abolish the monopoly. I would also write to the Commission for Racial Equality (CRE) and the Equal Opportunities Commission to ask for their support. I would write to the CRE first, since I noticed that its head and the Lord Chancellor would be sitting at the same table at the end of the week, at a conference on racism in the law. I would ask the CRE head to pass the Lord Chancellor a letter, which argued that the monopoly should be abolished, since it was likely to lead to indirect discrimination against members of minority ethnic groups.

Allen Labor kindly offered to help with the process of lobbying MPs and gaining support for abolition. Hans Hartwig would do the same. Tom Barker agreed to contact Garry Hart to put our point of view and to ask him to get the Lord Chancellor to consider the matter.

ACTION

I wrote the next day, 8 December 1998, to the CRE. I was delighted to hear back by a letter dated 16 December to say that the Lord Chancellor had not been able to attend the meeting, but the CRE had brought up the matter with him nonetheless. They agreed with me that there appeared to a strong possibility of indirect discrimination and they were asking for the monopoly to be ended.

I immediately wrote to the Equal Opportunities Commission, arguing that the closed nature of Scrivener recruitment was likely to indirectly discriminate against women. I did not mention my success with the CRE, thinking it best that the Equal Opportunities Commission make its decision on the facts, independent of any influence from the CRE. The Equal Opportunities Commission, after a little chasing, agreed to oppose the monopoly and write to the Lord Chancellor. I then contacted Stonewall, which campaigns for gay and lesbian rights, to argue the same case of indirect exclusion. I got their support too.

GARRY HART – GETTING TO THE LORD CHANCELLOR

After Christmas, I resolved to contact Garry Hart. I rang a couple of times without success, but finally spoke to him on the same day that Tom Barker of the ASN did, 5 January 1999. I expressed my concerns about the failure to abolish the monopoly and asked if he could take the matter up. I said I would fax him a letter with my arguments.

I sent that letter the next day, 6 January. I summarised the arguments against the monopoly and indicated the opposition of the CRE and the probability that the UK Government was in breach of EU law by permitting the continuance of the monopoly. In particular, I argued that Art 86 of the EU Treaty was being breached because, as the Government's own advisors had said, it was impossible for 30 Scrivener notaries to service the whole of London. I said that I reserved my right to sue for £350,000 a year damages. Labour could either support the Scriveners and defend the monopoly or stand up for its principles and abolish it. I was ready to send out over 1,000 letters on the issue. I wanted an answer by noon that Friday, 8 January 1999.

When I came into the office that Friday morning, I was unsure if I would get a response. But Garry Hart rang to say that he had seen the Lord Chancellor the day before and shown him my letter. The Lord Chancellor was very interested and had asked for the file to come to him immediately. I thanked Mr Hart and spoke to my allies in the ASN. At last, we were getting somewhere.

LOBBYING MPS

Meanwhile, I drafted my letter to all MPs. I decided that if the Lord Chancellor was going to adopt my amendment, then pressure on him to do so would make him look good when he responded to it. If he was undecided, pressure to abolish would help make up his mind. If he had decided not to abolish, then he deserved all the opposition I could organise.

I used the 'mail merge' facility on my word processor. I was lucky that I showed the first draft to a colleague, Philip Eldin-Taylor, since he immediately improved it for me. He suggested that the key points of the letter be contained in the first three paragraphs and kept to less than a page, including my request for action. The technical information about notaries should be kept as an annex. This cut the task for the reader down to size and made me focus on the precise issues. The letter took about 30 seconds to read and recited the essential facts – that is:

- the monopoly dated back to the Middle Ages and was still in force today;
- the Scriveners were a closed shop, with only about 30 notaries at any one time since 1880;
- other notaries, competent to act outside London, were committing a criminal offence if they acted as one inside London;
- the Government's own advisors were in favour of abolition, notably the Office of Fair Trading and the LCD.

I also asked the MP to act by:

- writing to the Lord Chancellor to ask him to abolish the monopoly;
- supporting my amendment to the Access to Justice Bill, which would do this;
- asking his or her colleagues to do the same.

The annex described the duties of a notary and pointed out that foreign notaries could now work in the monopoly area. It emphasised that the Faculty Office, responsible for regulating the profession, had said all notarial acts were the same and the Scriveners' monopoly was only a geographical one. Crucially, I argued that the Government's own advisors were against the monopoly, but the Government had not even announced the results of the consultation on abolition. There was also a potential damages claim worth millions of pounds.

Structure of the letter

The key points in the letter could be seen by anyone immediately. The problem MPs have is lack of time. I had to make the points fast enough to keep them interested, but with enough detail to make it convincing. I also needed immediate action. Any MP could write to the Lord Chancellor and every letter would be worth a fortune to our cause.

I wanted the letter to find supporters in every shade of political opinion. I thought that the free market thinkers would find the monopoly absurd, modernisers would find it ridiculous and socialists find it inequitable and indirectly discriminatory. The chauvinists would see no reason why foreigners could work in the monopoly area when UK lawyers could not. I had to touch on points with which everyone could identify, since I did not have the time or resources to send out individualised letters to 597 MPs.

I was saved the substantial cost of postage by Austin Mitchell MP's assistant, Tim Grewal. He kindly offered to put all the letters in the internal post to MPs in their post boxes at the House of Commons if I could get the letters delivered to him. I had them run off at work, stuffed them into envelopes on the evening of Sunday 10 January 1999 and took a half-day holiday on 11 January to take them up to the House of Commons. Parliament had returned from the Christmas break that same day.

LOBBYING THE LORDS

I realised on speaking to Tim that the Bill had actually started its passage in the House of Lords. Since it was sponsored by the Lord Chancellor, this was logical, but it goes to show that my knowledge of Parliamentary procedure was still a little sketchy.

I decided to lobby the Lords and got a list of their names from the Lords Information office. Luckily, this included a table showing their party affiliation and the number of times they had attended the House of Lords in the last session of Parliament. This was a vital bit of information. There were over 1,000 Lords able to sit, but very few who did attend the Lords on a regular basis. To concentrate efforts, I went through the list with a pen, ignoring anyone who had attended less than 150 times. That shortened the list a great deal. I then highlighted any spokespersons on legal affairs, former judges in the House of Lords and any solicitor peers (I found an article in the Law Society Gazette usefully summarising these). I then wrote the same letter I had to the MPs, with a twist. Since I was only targeting 40 Lords, I personalised the letters by asking them to have a word with the Lord Chancellor personally. In the then atmosphere of the Lords, I thought this to be a likely way that they would proceed. I also asked them to introduce my amendment.

I realise now that I was correct to do this. Each active Lord had a greater chance of getting an amendment listed than did his or her MP equivalent.

There was less formality in procedure, less acrimony in debate and more cross-benchers whose votes might be needed by the Government.

GATHERING SUPPORT

I sent most of the letters to the Lords on 18 January. I decided to follow up immediately by telephone calls. I began with the Lords' Conservative spokesperson on legal affairs, Lord Kingsland QC. It took several calls to make contact but, on Monday 25 February 1999, I had a return call from him. He said that he supported me and had spoken to the Lord Chancellor's private office. It seemed that the Lord Chancellor was going to adopt my amendment, but if the Lord Chancellor did not move the amendment, he would do so himself. Since he was the Conservative Party spokesperson in the Lords, I effectively had the support of the Conservative peers for abolition.

I was amazed at this success, but decided to lock it in by contacting Edward Garnier QC MP in the Commons. He was the Conservative Party spokesperson for legal affairs in the Commons. Again, it took several phone calls to get through, but Edward Garnier also confirmed his personal support for abolition and that of the Conservative Party in the Commons.

I then turned to the Liberal Democrats. They had no less than three spokespersons in the Lords. I contacted each of them. Two supported me, one of them, Lord Goodhart, deciding beforehand to write to the Scriveners for their comments. The third Liberal Democrat peer did not want to take an active part in abolition, since he was occupied in opposing the changes to legal aid, but he was not in favour of the monopoly. I decided not to press the point and simply confirm that he did not oppose his colleagues' point of view.

Lord Goodhart had informed me that he was writing to the Scriveners. I had anticipated that the intellectual heavyweights would want more legal argument than I had provided in the general letter to Lords and MPs. I had therefore prepared a detailed brief, which set out all my arguments. More importantly, it set out all the arguments that I thought the Scriveners would use and countered them, using their own words and documentary evidence. It was in the form of a brief by a solicitor to counsel which, since they were barristers, I thought they would appreciate. Lord Goodhart and Lord Lester then, for the Liberal Democrats, both supported abolition. I thought this should get the votes of the remaining Liberal Democrat peers on my side.

Again, I doubled back to the Commons. The Liberal Democrats had been the most supportive of all parties at the time of the Competition Bill. Allen Labor of the ASN had done a terrific job in getting them to support abolition then. I discussed the matter with him and we agreed to ask the Liberal Democrats who were already on our side, to ask their spokesperson on legal affairs, John Burnett, to make abolition official Liberal Democrat policy.

Both he and I and Hans Hartwig rang around to ask for support. I made a beeline for John Burnett. Although I never spoke to him, the message came back from his secretary that he had decided to support abolition of the monopoly.

Cross-bench support

I received kind letters of support from a cross-bench peer, Lord Valerian Freyberg and a former House of Lords judge, Lord Brightman. It could be argued that these were less important, but I suggest they were also helpful. Since these people had no political axe to grind, their advice was indicative to the Government that it was making the right decision.

Meanwhile in the Commons

Allen Labor had been keen to get action. He visited the Commons and got the Liberal Democrats to table an early day motion to ask what the Government was doing about abolition of the monopoly. Edward Garnier, for the Conservatives, tabled a written question on the same subject. Chris Mullin, the influential Labour MP who was head of the Home Affairs Select Committee, tabled a similar question. MP after MP, from all sides of the House, began to write in support. We gained a total of nearly 30 MPs who clearly were on our side.

GETTING THE DECISION – CONSULTATION

I talked again with Garry Hart to ask whether the Government had yet come to a decision. He was non-committal. I did not mention that Lord Kingsland had told me the Lord Chancellor was going to abolish the monopoly, since that had been said in confidence.

I gathered that any decision on abolition and, indeed, on most legislative proposals could not be announced unless and until all the relevant Government ministers and their departments had been circulated with the proposal for their comments. This was apparently to avoid duplication of effort. Another department might well be planning to do the same thing or might object, because the proposal would affect what it was planning to do.

Helping the Government decision making process

I decided to increase the pressure by faxing as many Government Ministers as I could think of, urging them to act. These were:

- the Secretary of State for Trade and Industry, because the monopoly was against the policy of open competition;
- the Minister for Equal Opportunities, since the monopoly seemingly promoted indirect discrimination;
- the Minister for Women, since women had apparently less chances to become a Scrivener than men;
- the Minister for Education, since the Scrivener examinations did not seem to be externally validated and seemed unfair (because you needed to be apprenticed to a Scrivener to take them).

To each, I suggested that Labour had a choice: support the old system or your principles of fairness and openness. I pointed out that damages were potentially payable. I knew that civil service sensitivity to embarrassment to ministers would mean that each fax would lead to a succession of memos to and from the LCD. Other departments would want to make sure that they were not going to be made fools of by any failure by the LCD. The upshot would be to make the notary file become a hot potato which had to be dealt with. It would now be impossible to ignore.

Friends, clients and strangers

I asked a lot of people to write in to the Lord Chancellor, asking for the end of the monopoly. I found his fax number in the Lords and distributed it freely. Colleagues, clients and friends did write in. I think their efforts were significant. It appeared that ordinary people were taking an interest in the issue. It was a bit like a true life story in a boys' magazine which I had once read. A soldier at a frontier fort found himself surrounded by attackers. All his fellow soldiers had been killed, so he propped up their bodies to cover their firing stations and ran round the fort, firing from various places. He managed to give the impression that he was not alone and survived until reinforcements came.

DISCUSSIONS WITH CIVIL SERVANTS

I discussed the campaign with the civil servants dealing with the case. I apologised for the amount of post they would receive, but said I saw the matter in the following way:

- arguments at the time of the Competition Bill had been about whether the amendment to abolish was within the scope of the Bill. There could be no argument about that with the Access to Justice Bill;

- each government tended to deal with the legal professions only once in each term of office. Labour would almost certainly be in government for two terms, but would only deal with lawyers once. There would never be a better time than now, in a Bill designed to get rid of outdated legal practices;

- Labour had a huge majority and could pass practically anything, provided it was uncontroversial. It might never have such a majority again;

- I would fight on forever to win. I had taken three years to get to this stage and, so far, nobody had produced a single argument that could justify the monopoly. Civil servants, Tory peers – all were against it. If the argument was about using time effectively, I could guarantee to waste much more Civil Service and Government time unless and until abolition occurred.

ABOLITION ANNOUNCED

On 1 February 1999, the Government announced the abolition. A press release dealt with the issue and stressed that the Government had fully considered all Scrivener arguments, but had not found them convincing. The battle was nearly over.

The amendment was introduced at Report Stage and was passed without any dissent whatsoever on 16 February 1999. The Government had such a majority in the Commons that it was now impossible for the amendment to fail, especially since all the major parties now had abolition as their policy.

Saying thank you

I wrote immediately to everybody who had helped to say thank you. I was delighted with the help we had received, often from the most unexpected sources.

Timing

I decided to draw up a flowchart of likely reactions by those in favour of the monopoly. I decided that this would likely involve:

(a) an attempt to increase qualifications for working in London. Control of the content of that education would be by Scriveners;

(b) an attempt to re-work the rules for the conduct of notaries, which would put Scriveners in a better position than non-Scriveners;

(c) an amendment to the Access to Justice Bill which would undermine abolition.

PRE-EMPTING THE FIGHTBACK

Since the second and third alternatives would require time, I thought the top priority was to forestall another increase in notarial qualifications. Since the Government amendment allowed all currently qualified notaries to work in the monopoly area, I thought it likely that the Faculty Office would contact the LCD to ask for permission to raise educational qualifications again.

I decided to write first. I wrote to the LCD, thanking them for the amendment and saying that I thought it likely that the Faculty Office would now be suggesting an increase in qualification requirements for notaries wishing to practise in London. If this was accepted, the work done in abolishing the monopoly would be undone, since the monopoly would be reinstated by the back door, through the influence the Scriveners exerted on setting the qualification requirements. I said that if this happened, I would set about the whole process again.

I received a reply from the LCD dated 2 March 1999. They said the Faculty Office had asked them whether they wanted the Master of the Faculties to impose some special training requirement on notaries wishing to practise in London. The LCD had replied that the Government did not expect or wish him to impose higher standards of qualification in the City, any more than the Master of the Faculties imposed higher standards on notaries wishing to practise in Birmingham. People could join the Scriveners Company if they wished, but it should not be a legal obligation.

In a word, the Scriveners had lost. The reaction of the LCD shows the value of getting the Government to adopt the amendment. Now, it would be the will of the Government that was being thwarted; abolition had become the new status quo.

RETALIATION IN THE COMMONS

Each Bill has to go through the same stages in the Commons that it undergoes in the Lords, that is, First, Second and Third Readings, and Report and Committee stages. I saw on the parliamentary website that Sir Nicholas Lyell, the Conservative Shadow Attorney General, had commented in Parliament, during the Second Reading of the Bill, that the Government had acted too hastily in abolishing the monopoly. The concern he had was the maintenance of standards. He was in favour of a proposal whereby non-Scrivener notaries would have to make it clear that they did not have the same level of qualifications as Scriveners. His colleague, Edward Garnier, would raise the matter at Committee stage. I wrote to both of them immediately and to each member of the Committee with my objections. Sir Nicholas Lyell admitted (after seeing my letter, comparing the educational qualifications of Scrivener and non-Scrivener notaries) that the Scriveners may have over-stated their case. Edward Garnier was careful to make clear he would not be raising the matter and had not changed his opinion on the monopoly since he last spoke to me. He indicated that Peter Brooke MP would be raising the matter personally at Report Stage on behalf of his Scrivener constituents.

Peter Brooke's amendment

I wrote to Peter Brooke to ask him what he intended to do. I wanted to know if he was going to move an amendment or not, and what it would contain. I never got a clear answer and decided that this therefore meant he would be moving one.

His chances of success were minimal, but I decided that, having come this far, I was not going to fail at the last hurdle. I got the names of all the Whips of each main party and wrote to each of them, asking them to oppose the amendment.

Since Peter Brooke refused to say what his amendment would say or what arguments he had for introducing it, I had to proceed by guesswork until the last moment. Peter Brooke tabled his amendment on the last day possible. Although I was in France at the time, I got the gist of it by telephone from the Public Bills Office at the House of Commons. The amendment proposed the creation of a new criminal offence. It said that:

> No person shall take or use any name, title or description implying that he is certificated as a notary by the Incorporated Company of Scriveners of London unless he is qualified to practise as a Scrivener notary in accordance with the rules and ordinances of that Company.

Infringement would be a criminal offence, punishable by a fine of up to level 3 on the standard scale for fines (£2,000). I made the following objections both to the Whips and the LCD:

- saying that you were a Scrivener when you were not would be a breach of professional conduct rules. The criminal offence was therefore unnecessary, since a notary in default could be prevented from practising by the Faculty Office;

- no reason had been given as to why the new offence was needed, despite repeated requests for justification;

- the public was already protected against unqualified persons practising as notaries by s 10 of the Public Notaries Act 1843, which imposed the same fine. No further protection of the public was therefore needed. Other notaries were equally competent to act. The amendment was simply there to protect the commercial interests of Scrivener notaries;

- the proposed offence was extremely vague. Would a notary who said he or she was at least as competent to act as a Scrivener be committing an offence? Would to say that one was a notary and practised in London 'imply' that one was a Scrivener notary?;

- Scriveners could rely on the law of passing off to protect themselves against people pretending to be Scriveners. However, there was no known case of this ever happening;

- since it appeared that the supposed reason for the amendment was that of different notarial qualifications, I summarised my arguments that Scriveners were not better qualified and could be argued to be worse qualified than general notaries. The Government had accepted that general notaries were perfectly competent to act when it moved the amendment to abolish the Bill. The Scriveners had produced no new evidence (and, certainly, none they seemed ready to publish) for their alleged superior skills. I asked the Whips to co-ordinate opposition to the amendment.

The ASN

The active members of the ASN also contacted MPs and the LCD. They raised further arguments, notably that Scrivener clients were usually sophisticated ones, such as banks and City solicitors, who were quite capable of making informed decisions.

The vote

The amendment was raised in the Commons by Peter Brooke. He did not have much to say in favour of his amendment which seemed at all relevant. His central argument was that protection was needed for the name of Scrivener since, otherwise, foreign clients might get confused and cease to use notarial services in London. The Government rejected the amendment. It argued that:

(a) the Scriveners could always advertise that they were members of the Company;

(b) Scrivener clients were not uninformed. They could always ring the Company to check if somebody was a Scrivener or not;

(c) the Trade Descriptions Act 1968 already made it an offence to make false or misleading statements about services;

(d) the titles 'barrister' and 'legal executive' were not protected in this way. 'Solicitor' was a protected title, but all solicitors were covered by this, not just one group of them;

(e) there was no hard evidence that non-Scriveners provided a lesser service than Scriveners. The Faculty Office had said all notaries were qualified to do all notarial acts.

Peter Brooke then withdrew the amendment. He had achieved nothing, save a public statement by the Government that there was no hard evidence that Scrivener notaries were better than other notaries.

Revising the notarial practice rules

The Faculty Office decided to consult on new notarial practice rules. These contained a proposal to make falsely claiming to be a Scrivener notary a breach of professional conduct. Interestingly, the Notaries' Society objected to this, along with the ASN and myself. The rule was passed nonetheless. I decided that, since the last thing I wanted to do was to claim to be a Scrivener, I would concentrate on making sure that abolition was brought into force as soon as possible.

BRINGING THE ACCESS TO JUSTICE BILL INTO EFFECT

Many Bills are complicated and can only be brought into effect in stages. The Access to Justice Bill was one of these. But, although some provisions of the Bill needed time for implementation – the setting up quangos, etc – the abolition of the monopoly required nothing.

Therefore, the ASN and I wrote to the LCD to press for implementation of the new Act as soon as possible. There is a conventional two month delay after Royal Assent to a Bill. Consent to the Access to Justice Bill was given on 28 July 1999. The earliest abolition could occur was therefore 28 September 1999. The Faculty Office decided that it wanted 1 November 1999, since this would fit in with the issue of new practising certificates to notaries. We decided not to press the point and 1 November 1999 was the date in which the notarial monopoly of the Scriveners came to an end.

CONCLUSION

It had been necessary to fight right down to the end, but we had come out with the result we wanted. I decided that, now the English notarial profession was in compliance with common sense and EU law, it was time to resume my attacks on the notarial monopolies in Europe. Hopefully, all English notaries would be able to support me in gaining work abroad. That, however, is the subject of another book.

Personally, I had found the struggle to abolish the monopoly an interesting challenge. At university, I had studied some sociology. I had been interested by the question of what place the individual still had in this world. It seemed to me now that it was still a significant one. A small number of people had changed the notarial profession forever.

I have since asked myself whether abolition could have been achieved earlier. Perhaps we would have been better off going for abolition without any of the earlier work on abolishing restrictions for European notaries. Perhaps the Conservative Government could have been pushed to abolish the monopoly in the last days of the Major Government. I think now that we could have succeeded even then.

PARLIAMENTARY PROCEDURE
AND INFORMATION

The best indepth guide for the general reader is Silk, P and Walters, L, *How Parliament Works*, 4th edn, 1998, Longman. There are specialist works, such as Erskine May, treating of procedure in great detail. My own view is that, in lobbying, one needs to have a good grasp of the principles of procedure, but over-concentration on minute detail kills impetus.

An excellent source of information is the Houses of Parliament website located at: **www.parliament.uk**

It contains the full text of *Hansard* (the official transcript of everything that is said in Parliament) and details of forthcoming House business in both the Lords and the Commons, together with the full text of Bills and proposed amendments to them. The site is indexed (click on 'Index' on the welcoming page or 'Site Map') and contains a lot of downloadable material, ranging from details of the names and constituencies of MPs and Lords and House of Commons Information Office factsheets (abbreviated to HCIO on the site), which explain parliamentary procedure and most frequently asked questions. Indeed, the information on MPs contains links to websites of MPs and email connections (reach this by clicking on 'House of Commons', then 'Information about the House of Commons and Members of Parliament'). If you scroll to the end of the index and click on 'Search', you can enter keywords and will be given a list of occasions on which that keyword has come up in the Houses of Parliament. I found this site invaluable during the campaign, as it is updated daily. There are occasional lapses in the updating, however, so I also used the human based guides to Parliament.

LORDS AND COMMONS INFORMATION OFFICE

You can contact these simply by ringing the Houses of Parliament on 020 7219 3000 and asking to be put through. The direct line for the House of Commons Public Information Office is 020 7219 4272. For the House of Lords Information Office, the number is 020 7219 3107. They will send you a current list of MPs and Lords through the post. There is no charge. I found this easier than downloading a list from the website.

The information you get varies a little in quality. Straightforward enquiries are easily dealt with. However, I found that information about recently tabled amendments could take a while to get through to the Information Offices. For this, I used the Public Bills Offices of the Lords and the Commons.

PUBLIC BILLS OFFICE

Both the Lords and the Commons have a Public Bills Office, which is in charge of the passage of Public Bills through the respective House. It is staffed by various clerks and support staff. I found that once you had located which clerk was dealing with your Bill, you could get an up to the minute account of what was happening.

The Public Bills Offices are not involved in the formulation of government policy on the Bill. Theirs is an organisational function. Even their best guess as to when a Bill will be debated can be wrong, since the Government may decided to speed up or slow down the progress of a Bill for tactical reasons.

OTHER USEFUL BOOKS ON PARLIAMENT

Vacher's Parliamentary Companion (Vacher Dod Publishing Ltd, published quarterly) has a complete list of MPs, Lords, Scottish Members of Parliament and Welsh and Northern Irish Assembly members. It has a lot of fascinating details on all party groups, the names and areas of responsibility of ministers, senior civil servants and much more besides. It is updated quarterly. I did not use it, but this was simply from ignorance.

Dod's Parliamentary Companion (Vacher Dod Publishing Ltd) is published every year and contains details of MPs and peers and their political interests. The information is supplied by the MPs and peers, so should be taken with a little salt. I never used this, but some may find it helpful. At least a professed interest is a starting point for contact.

Roth, A and Criddle, B, *Parliamentary Profiles*, 1997–2002, Parliamentary Profiles, continually updated: this has now been updated by adding a new volume for the 1997 intake of MPs. It is in four volumes, which cost a substantial amount each. I never used this, but it does contain details of MPs and peers, as well as their voting records and careers.

GENERAL POINT

I found that some of the advice I read in other books on lobbying did not accord with my own experience. For example, some suggest that you should carefully research the interests of MPs and target those who are most likely to support you. I certainly think this seems a good idea, but I simply did not have the time to do it. I wrote to every MP on the basis that I needed a few who would act. All the sympathy in the world will not work unless the MP actually takes steps to help you. Nonetheless, even the cheaper guides, like *Vacher's Parliamentary Companion*, can give a lot of clues. Those actively involved in areas because of their personal interest as shown by membership of all party subject groups or because they are involved in government or opposition policy making on the issues that concern you are obviously people to spend extra time on. The parliamentary website lists which MPs belong to all party interest groups (if they are an office holder) and individual MPs' websites give further information (also accessible via the parliamentary website). On the other hand, if you spend so much time analysing the politicians that you never ask them to act, you will never get anywhere.

See Appendix 2 for protocol on approaching MPs.

APPROACHING AND USING MPs

Parliament is a place governed by conventions. One of these is that MPs are not supposed to concern themselves with the affairs of a constituent of another MP. If an MP receives correspondence from another MP's constituent, the MP receiving the letter is supposed to forward it to the correct MP

Luckily, I knew nothing of this when I wrote, and simply contacted every MP. I consider the rule to be a relic of the days when the public was not supposed to be concerned about national issues, but only their private ones. It seems to me that, if taken literally, one's freedom to lobby disappears.

Thankfully, by no means all MPs take such a parochial view of their interests. However, their chief duty is still to their constituents, who send in a lot of post. Since an MP's time is therefore precious, letters have to be kept brief. To maximise the benefit of help from MPs, I suggest the following, from my experience and pointers from other lobbying books (which are summarised in Appendix 5):

- keep letters short, with any technical information in an annex. No more than three sides of A4 paper in all, preferably less. You simply write to the MP by name at the House of Commons, London SW1A 0AA;

- contact your own constituency MP first to get them on board. My own MP at the time, Diane Abbott, was immensely helpful in getting replies. Your MP will also receive letters from other MPs about the issue and it is polite to keep your MP informed;

- get as many people as possible writing to MPs. The more post they get, the more they consider it to be an issue;

- ask for specific action, something the MP can do now. The simplest is to get them to ask a question of the minister responsible for your matter. This way, both the MP you have contacted and the Government are alerted to the issue;

- deal with the contrary arguments, making sure you can refute them. Remember, your letter may be the first communication your MP contact receives on the issue. You need to supply him or her with the ammunition necessary to counter opposition;

- it is good to get letters arriving from different people at different times to keep the pressure up;

- make sure your information is accurate;

- you can contact MPs by telephone simply by ringing the House of Commons on 020 7219 3000. Since MPs are often elsewhere in Parliament, you can leave a message with their assistant or secretary or the House of Commons' own message service. I thought it polite to write first, asking for help and saying that I would ring;

- keep all replies and note any reference on the return letter from an MP. Use it if you write again. MPs have so much correspondence, they need to file it and if there is a quiet period in your campaign, your file may be sent to storage;

- your own constituency MP can often be most easily met at their surgery meetings, when they are available to meet constituents. Often, MPs are in London from Monday to Thursday and hold surgery meetings back in their constituency on a Friday or Saturday. You should be able to find out details of when and where these meetings are at your local library or by phoning your MP at the House of Commons. It is best to make an appointment.

WHAT CAN MPS BE USED FOR?

It is important to be clear that, although the MP will help you, you can equally be helping them. If you can provide information and back up which gives the MP good publicity, he or she gets the opportunity to get more of the limelight and impress the Whips and fellow colleagues. The things they do for you are also an opportunity for them. Specifically, an MP can help you by the following methods.

Getting answers to questions put to ministers

Written questions in Parliament

Written questions are a source of information that you may have great difficulty getting on your own. The answers to written questions are in *Hansard* and can be found on the parliamentary website. The information will not be given if obtaining it requires a disproportionate cost or is simply unavailable. The answers will be researched by civil servants. Like all government produced information, it is impossible for the Government to deny its accuracy, so the answer produced may be very helpful to your cause. Each MP can ask an unlimited number of written questions in each session. The format is prescribed by convention and the question (like oral questions) must be tabled in advance to the House of Commons table office. The clerks there will assist MPs in making sure the questions are put correctly.

Questions must:

- be addressed to the senior minister in the department whose responsibility the matter is;
- be put to each department responsible separately if there is more than one department responsible;
- seek information;
- not concern national security or information which is deemed to be commercially sensitive.

The response time to written questions is about a week.

Oral questions in Parliament

These, again, must be tabled in advance. Since there are so many of them, the best chance of getting a question answered is to ask it as early as possible. This are two calendar weeks before the next date that that department answers questions. A rota system means that each department, for example, the Department of Trade and Industry, answers questions about once a month. The time allowed is about an hour each day, from Monday to Thursday, starting after prayers at 2.30 pm. MPs are limited to asking no more than eight oral questions a fortnight, with a maximum of two a day.

Any question tabled goes into a lucky dip known as the five o'clock shuffle (so called because it takes place at that time). Only the first 16 or so picked are likely to be answered in the time allowed. When the minister reads out his or her prepared answer on the appointed day, the MP who asked the question can ask a supplementary question. This, by convention, must be on the same matter or a related one. The Speaker is allowed at this point to call on MPs to ask further supplementary questions, especially if the MP has known expertise or interest in the subject. If several MPs ask essentially the same question, they can all be invited by the Speaker to put a supplementary question.

The answer to the questions is of course in the text of *Hansard*. The questions are set out in the order paper for the day. Both can be found on the parliamentary website.

Prime Minister's Question Time

This is basically a variant of departmental question time, with the variation that the main question is usually an innocent one about the Prime Minister's appointments for a particular day, with the real question put as a supplementary. It now occurs once a week.

Introducing new Bills under the Private Member's Bill procedure

There are, in fact, three ways to do this, discussed in detail in Appendix 4.

Tabling Early Day Motions

An Early Day Motion (usually shortened to EDM) is a motion tabled for debate 'on an early day'. The fact is that very few of the 1,000 or so motions tabled in a parliamentary session will never be debated and the MPs tabling them know it.

The idea is to canvass support and show the Government that MPs are concerned about the issue. EDMs are listed on the parliamentary website, with a running total, showing how many MPs have signed them. The motion must only be one sentence long, although this is often sidestepped by making the sentence very long.

The MP tables the motion by handing it to the table office. Each EDM is given a number and this should be noted, so that one can encourage MPs to sign it. It is listed in the notice paper (or 'blues'), which is part of the daily bundle of papers (called the vote bundle or simply 'the vote') received by MPs. The EDM appears the day after it is tabled, then, for the next two weeks, it is reprinted each time more MPs add their names to it. After two weeks, it is only reprinted each Thursday. The names of a maximum of six original sponsors are reprinted each time the EDM is, with the names of any new sponsors that day. To maximise support, it is a good idea to make sure the original sponsors are from all parties, if possible, and are the kind of MPs who will help you get further support.

Opinion is divided on how useful EDMs are. At least they can help find further supporters you can use for other work in the Commons.

Speeding up replies to your letters

Parliamentary protocol ensures that if an MP writes to a minister, the minister will write back. This can be helpful but, on the other hand, a reply is not always an answer. It can easily be a 'the Government is considering the matter and will give its reply in due course' type of letter.

Having said that, the response to an MP will certainly be faster than to your own letters. This is provided for in internal Civil Service guidelines. There is also much more chance that the minister will personally read the letter rather than have it read and answered for him, although many letters are effectively answered by civil servants and only signed by the minister. Similarly, you will find that many people who forget to reply to your letters suddenly remember them when they are sent in with an MP's request for a reply.

Contacts and persuasion in their party and Parliament

People are often more easily convinced by those they know than any amount of rational argument. MPs will all have contacts and friends they can influence on a personal level, both within and across party.

I asked advice from a contact before I lobbied MPs about the best way to go about it. My contact had lobbied very effectively on a sensitive issue. His advice was to find sympathetic MPs and use them to convince those they knew who were waverers. Unsympathetic people should simply be ignored. I think this is the best and simplest advice I ever had on the subject.

The fact that one's own backbenchers are concerned is a reason for any government to be concerned. Party disunity is bad for morale, effectiveness and election victories. Concern does not have to be pushed to the point of rebellion. Simply taking the time to raise the issue with the minister concerned in private correspondence can also be very effective.

Arranging meetings in the House of Commons

There are cafés and restaurants in the House of Commons where you can meet MPs informally and my colleague, Allen Labor, found this useful as a means of getting to know them.

Speaking on adjournment debates and other motions

Adjournment debates

At the close of business each parliamentary day, there is an adjournment debate. Literally, this is on whether or not the House should adjourn until the next day. In fact, the debate is an opportunity for backbench MPs to raise matters of concern to them.

The debate lasts half an hour. The MP speaks first for about 15 minutes, leaving 15 minutes for the minister's reply. The debate can be on any subject, but cannot request legislation. There is a competition by ballot for the right to speak. MPs apply to the Speaker's office by the Wednesday evening of the preceding week. The next day, the results of the ballot are announced. However, the Speaker can choose who should speak on one of the adjournment debates each week. The debate can be a quiet affair, since it is possible that everyone save the Speaker, the minister and the MP will have left the Chamber, but it is a chance to get matters raised and recorded in *Hansard*.

Four times a year, on the days before the parliamentary holidays begin (at Christmas, Easter, Whitsun and summer), there is a whole day of adjournment debates. The right to speak is again decided by ballot.

Three times a year, there are Consolidated Fund debates, which run through the night and in which subjects are suggested by private members and chosen by ballot. These tend to be longer debates, but competition to speak is again intense.

Opposition days

The opposition has the right to set the agenda on a few days per year, but usually knows exactly what it wishes to raise, leaving little room for pressure groups.

THE STAGES A BILL PASSES THROUGH IN PARLIAMENT

For the lobbyist, every stage is a good one, save for Third Reading in the Commons, since no amendments are permitted then. The stages are broadly similar in each House and are as follows.

FIRST READING

The First Reading of a Bill is the time it is introduced into Parliament. The Bill is not, in fact, read, but simply produced to the House. Each Bill is sponsored by an MP, known as 'the member in charge'. Usually, this is the Government Minister in charge of the Department of State which has produced the Bill. So, for the Access to Justice Bill, where the Bill was produced by the LCD, the Lord Chancellor was the member in charge and the Bill was introduced in the House of Lords, since that is where the Lord Chancellor sits.

Usually, government Bills start their passage through Parliament in the Commons. The member in charge gives notice of the Bill's long and short titles (which tell the public and Parliament what the Bill is going to do when enacted) and of the Government's intention to introduce the Bill at a specified date. When that day arrives, the Speaker asks the member in charge to bring a 'dummy Bill' (a document which simply notes the long and short titles of the Bill and a list of no more than a dozen MPs who support it) to the Table of the House. The Bill's short title is then read out by the Clerk of the House. The Bill is then said to have had its First Reading. It is ordered that the Bill be printed and read a second time at a date to be fixed.

If a Bill has already been through all its stages in the Lords, then the formal First Reading in the Commons is dispensed with. Taxation and some finance Bills can be introduced by order of the House. So can 10 Minute Rule Bills, which we will discuss later. In these cases too, there is no formal first reading.

The Bill must be printed in full before it can go any further. This is normally done within 24 hours of its introduction (in the case of government Bills). Private Member's Bills can take longer.

Explanatory memorandum

A short memorandum is attached to all government Bills and to many Private Member's Bills. The purpose is to explain why the Bill has been introduced and what its implications are for government finances and public service manpower.

The Second Reading normally follows 10 days or so after the First Reading. The date can be discovered from the parliamentary website or by telephoning the Public Bills Office for the Commons (or the Lords, if that is where the Bill was introduced).

SECOND READING

This is the debate on the principles of the Bill, including matters MPs feel should have been put in the Bill or left out of it. However, detailed consideration or discussion of individual clauses is not possible. The amount of time given for Second Reading debates varies. It can be given several days if the matter is highly important or controversial, but, normally, a major government Bill will be allocated one day from around 4 pm to 10 pm. Private Member's Bills are heard on Fridays between 9.30 am and 2.30 pm. Less important Bills get less time. Some matters which are not controversial can avoid a Second Reading altogether, that is, they pass this stage without any debate at all. Other non-controversial Bills can receive their Second Reading in a Standing Committee, rather than on the floor of the House. The distinction is that most Second Readings take place in the Chamber of the Commons and that, therefore, it is open to any MP to take part in the debate. In Standing Committee, on the other hand, only those MPs who are members of that Committee can take part.

The Second Reading is a time where opposition to the Bill can be voiced and increasingly has been used by government backbenchers to show their disagreement with government policy. It is still rare for governments to lose a Bill at this stage, because of the majorities they have and the discipline exerted by the party Whips, but vocal opposition at this stage sends a signal to the Government and it has still got plenty of time to amend its own Bill in response to pressure.

COMMITTEE

The Committee Stage of a Bill usually occurs at least 10 days after the Second Reading. As with most time indications in Parliament, this is purely conventional. The idea is simply to let people have time to comment and react. Up to now, the Bill has had no detailed examination at all. Committees do this job. They are of three kinds:

(a) Committees of the Whole House;

(b) Standing Committees; and

(c) Select Committees (since this is very rarely used, I will not be discussing it).

Committees of the Whole House

These used to be the normal procedure, but is now confined to three situations:

- uncontroversial Bills, which can thus go through Committee stage in minutes. The majority of Bills treated by a Committee of the Whole House are of this type;

- extremely urgent Bills;

- Bills of 'first class constitutional importance'. Like many conventions in Parliament, this does not have an exact scope. Bills on accession to the EEC and devolution have been considered in this way. Presumably, if a republic was proposed, this would also be considered of first class importance, but whether a particular Bill is of this type is a matter for debate.

The Committee of the Whole House meets in the Chamber of the House of Commons. The only difference in procedure is that the House is presided over by the Chairman of Ways and Means, not the Speaker. The Chairman sits at the table next to the clerk, not in the Speaker's chair, and the mace is put under the table, not on top of it.

Standing Committees

The name 'Standing Committee' is not accurate. For each Bill, their composition changes. There is no restriction on the number of Standing Committees which can exist at any one time. The MPs nominated to them are chosen by the Committee of Selection, consisting of senior MPs and Whips. Committees tend to have around 16–50 members, with most having numbers in the 20s.

The Committee of Selection seeks to balance the composition of each standing committee so that each of the major parties is fairly represented (that is, having the same proportion of members as they have in the House of Commons) and that MPs who have particular interest or expertise in an area can have a chance to contribute.

The Government will always have at least one minister on the Committee and one of its Whips. The main opposition parties will each have a frontbencher and a Whip. The rest of the committee will be made up of MPs interested in the issue and, in the case of the Government, those whose loyalty to government policy is assured.

Meeting procedure

Bills sent to Standing Committees are often said to have been 'sent upstairs', because the Committees meet in the committee rooms on the first floor of the House of Commons, on the side facing the river. The public can attend and all proceedings are noted in *Hansard* and can be found on the parliamentary website.

They usually work from 10.30 am until 1 pm on Tuesdays and Thursdays, and, if the matter is controversial, continue from 4.30 pm until they stop. At the latest, this must be by 1 pm on the following day. The Bill is considered clause by clause. Any Committee member can suggest amendments and this stage presents probably the best opportunity for lobbyists to get amendments accepted or their objections to proposed legislation heard.

However, the selection of the amendments which are debated is at the discretion of the Chairman of the Committee, who also relies on the following conventions in choosing whether or not to accept the amendments proposed:

- amendments must be 'within the scope of the Bill', that is, its purpose as defined in its long title;
- they must be relevant;
- they must not be wrecking amendments;
- they cannot be vague or unintelligible;
- they cannot conflict with previous Committee decisions;
- they cannot create a public charge, unless the House has previously approved the money for this.

WHO PUTS FORWARD AMENDMENTS AND WHY?

The Government moves many amendments itself at Committee stage. This is because:

- the Bill may have been drafted in a hurry and only on reflection by the Government or its civil servants does it realise that the Bill either fails to do what it should or has undesirable consequences;

- pressure from outside groups, its own backbenchers, the opposition parties, the public or the media may lead it to yield to criticism and withdraw parts of the Bill or change it;
- some amendments are technical ones, simply designed to improve the drafting of the Bill.

The opposition parties have their own political agenda and will often seek to criticise and attack the Government by proposing amendments. Backbenchers move amendments, often after being encouraged to do so by outside pressure groups.

In Paul Silk's excellent book on Parliament, *How Parliament Works*, he refers to the fact that backbenchers are on very unequal terms when they try to propose amendments, as opposed to the Government. The statistics indicate that only one in 20 of backbencher amendments are accepted. The reason is that the Government has the entire resources of the Civil Service and a disciplined political party behind it, while the backbencher has a crowded diary and a very small and under-resourced team to back him or her up. Additionally, if the Bill or matter is a controversial one, the Government often resorts to the procedure known as the guillotine to drastically cut down the time for debate. Nonetheless, the time a Bill spends in Committee can be the best opportunity for a lobbyist to make an impact. The numbers are smaller and there is a better chance of finding people who are interested in and informed about your issue.

The amount of time a Bill takes at Committee stage varies and one needs to check with the Public Bills Office in the Commons what the allotted time is. One finds this varies, according to the rest of the Government's timetable and whether its legislative programme is going as planned. Major Bills can take several weeks, but it is important to note that even this time passes quickly. If intervention is planned by way of amendment, it needs to be very timely.

REPORT STAGE

After Committee Stage, the Bill as amended comes back to the whole House of Commons for consideration as amended. This stage is called 'consideration stage', but is usually referred to as Report Stage. All MPs can speak at Report Stage and further amendments can be moved. The Speaker is in the chair and selects which amendments are to be heard. Again, there are conventions governing what can be moved at Report Stage. Matters already discussed at Committee Stage cannot be moved again as amendments.

This stage is an opportunity to consider the Bill as a whole, so debate does not proceed through the Bill on a clause by clause basis. Since many Bills start their life together, at the beginning of each new parliamentary session in

November, it is often the case that, by Easter, many Bills will be reaching Report Stage at about the same time. The time taken at Report Stage is rarely more than two sittings (that is, days) However, since all amendments drawn for debate have to be discussed and voted on, these sittings may well go on until very late at night.

For the lobbyist, the Report Stage presents the last opportunity in the Commons to get amendments moved.

THIRD READING

The Bill as amended at Report Stage comes back to the whole House of Commons for its last stage there. The Third Reading is usually a short debate which occasionally results in a vote. The Government can lose the Bill even at this stage, but rarely does. No amendments can be made in the Commons at this stage. The Bill then passes to the Lords to repeat essentially the same stages.

The House of Lords

Procedure in the House of Lords is similar to that of the House of Commons. There is a formal First Reading, a debate at the Second Reading on the general principles of the Bill, an opportunity for amendments and a detailed clause by clause analysis at Committee Stage and Report Stage and further consideration and amendments at the Third Reading. But there are also differences:

- in the Lords, all stages are taken on the floor of the House. There is no equivalent of the Bill being 'sent upstairs', as Bills are at Committee Stage in the Commons;
- the Chairman does not select amendments. All amendments set down may be debated;
- there is no guillotine procedure, so the Government cannot cut off debate without consent;
- amendments can be put at the Third Reading, but not on matters which have been fully debated and decided on at an earlier stage in the Lords;
- the Government has no absolute right to put its business in priority to that of other peers. In fact, the Government is given priority, but much more time is made for Private Member's Bills in the Lords;
- the same lack of formal priority for the Government gives persistent peers much better chances of getting their point of view across than exists for a backbencher in the Commons;

- the lack of dependence on a party Whip encourages political independence. This has meant that the Lords has tended to become the place where the Government is most likely to be defeated in Parliament. Although the Government can reverse this defeat in the Commons, it may be tempted to revise its proposals, or even drop them, in order to save parliamentary time.

DISAGREEMENT BETWEEN THE COMMONS AND THE LORDS

If there is no disagreement between the Houses, the Bill can go for Royal Assent. But if one House objects to part of a Bill and makes amendments to it, then those amendments must be considered by the House which first approved the Bill. The rest of the Bill does not need to be considered.

If the amendments are accepted, then the Bill can go for Royal Assent. If not, the amendments will either be overturned and the Bill sent back or a compromise will be suggested. Sometimes, amendments go backwards and forwards several times. Usually, disagreements are ironed out, otherwise the Bill would be lost.

ROYAL ASSENT

Once both Houses have passed the Bill, it goes for Royal Assent. This is automatic, but there is often a delay between granting of Royal Assent and the coming into force of the Act (as the Bill is now called). There is a conventional period of two months between Royal Assent and implementation, but it is possible that implementation may be delayed further. Often, Acts contain a 'commencement clause', which provides that the relevant Secretary of State may, by order at a future date, bring part or all of the Act into force. Implementation can be staggered over years or may never happen.

PRIVATE MEMBER'S BILLS

Private Members' Bills can be introduced in three ways:

(a) under the presentation procedure;

(b) under the 10 Minute Rule;

(c) via the ballot.

PRESENTATION PROCEDURE BILLS

Any MP can introduce a Bill after having given due notice, but such Bills are lower in parliamentary priority than Ballot Bills. They stand no chance of becoming law unless they are completely uncontroversial. Bills put forward in this way are usually promoted to publicise a cause.

Ten Minute Rule Bills

These Bills are also often not genuinely aimed at changing the law, but at 'raising consciousness' of the issue. From the seventh week of every parliamentary session, on every Tuesday and Wednesday, just before the main business of the day begins, one MP is allowed to make a 10 Minute speech promoting a Bill. If the proposal is objected to, a 10 minute speech against the Bill is heard. The proposal is then voted on. Assuming the vote is won, the MP's Bill can progress.

In fact, the Bill has very little chance of becoming law and only about 25 10 Minute Rule Bills have become law since 1945. The system remains popular with MPs, since it brings them publicity. The Bill is heard when the House is full of MPs and journalists and gives them the satisfaction of having introduced a Bill (although not necessarily the greater one of having it passed). 15 sitting days' notice have to be given to introduce a 10 Minute Rule Bill and the right to do so is given on a 'first come, first served' basis. Notice has to be given to the Public Bill Office and MPs often camp out all night to be sure to be first in the queue.

THE BALLOT

A ballot is held shortly after the beginning of each session of Parliament. Over 400 MPs usually enter, but only 20 numbers are drawn, ranked in order of drawing. Because of the limited time available for Private Member's Bills, only the first six drawn can introduce Bills which are at all controversial if they want to be certain of progressing to the Second Reading. On the other hand, Bills lower in ranking may get through, but only if enough time is left and they are non-controversial.

For those MPs who come high in the ballot, there will be many offers of subjects for legislation. Both pressure groups and government Whips will contact them, in the hope of getting parliamentary time. For the MP, the attraction of tacit government support is that the Government is much more likely to make extra time available to pass the Bill if necessary. Additionally, helping the Government implement more of its programme is a plus point for the MP seeking eventual government office.

There is a good deal of chance with regard to whether an MP chooses one subject rather than another. Austin Mitchell MP decided to introduce a Bill to remove the monopoly solicitors had over conveyancing after receiving representations to him by the Consumers Association, but he has since made it clear that he did not know, until the last moment, whether he would choose that Bill or another one on an entirely different subject.

PROCEDURE CONCERNING PRIVATE MEMBER'S BILLS

In the Commons, government business has priority. Private Member's Bill are allotted between 10 and 13 Fridays. The time constraints are therefore very tight, since Private Member's Bills must pass through all the same stages as any other Bill, but with less time allowed.

Friday is a particularly difficult day, since it is one on which many MPs choose to return to their constituencies. The Parliamentary day is from 9.30 am to 2.30 pm. In order to ensure that the Bill passes through the Second Reading stage, the promoters of the Bill need to 'secure the closure', which means getting 100 votes in favour of the motion to close debate on the Bill and winning the division itself. This will entail extensive lobbying, since the natural tendency of MPs will be to drift away on Fridays to their constituencies, not stay to the end to support the Bill. If closure is not obtained, then debate is adjourned and the Bill loses its priority in the list.

Assuming the Bill does pass Second Reading, it goes to Committee Stage. When it returns to Report Stage, even greater problems await. Each amendment moved must be debated and closure on each must be achieved, with 100 votes in favour of closure. Often, Bills are simply 'talked out' by the tabling of spurious amendments, which use up precious time. MPs may decide to table amendments to one Bill, not because they oppose it, but because they wish to ensure that there is no time left to discuss the next Bill on the list.

Once a Bill has gone through all stages in the Commons, it has to pass through the Lords like any other Bill. Detailed discussion of the procedure can be found in:

- Silk, P and Walters, R, *How Parliament Works*, 4th edn, 1998, Longman; and
- in the House of Commons Factsheet No 4, available from the parliamentary website.

USEFULNESS OF PRIVATE MEMBER'S BILLS

The number of Bills passed is small in total and most are uncontroversial. However, controversial Bills do get passed or, at least, show the Government that there is serious feeling about the issue. Bills may even be withdrawn, but on a government promise to deal with the issue itself. It has to be remembered that the abolition of capital punishment, the legalisation of abortion and homosexuality and the abolition of theatre censorship were all matters promoted by Private Member's Bills. More recently, successful Bills have increased access to information and improved rights for the disabled.

OTHER BOOKS ON LOBBYING

I include here a list of books on this subject, with a further list of their points of interest by way of a list of their highlights. The book can be divided into 3 classes:

(a) books by lobbyists on their experiences, giving ideas on how to do likewise;

(b) books by professional lobbyists about the profession of lobbyist and directories of lobbyists and lobbying groups;

(c) sociological/political books about the role of pressure groups in society and the process of social change.

'HOW TO DO IT' BOOKS BY PEOPLE WITH EXPERIENCE

- Wilson, D, *Pressure: The A to Z of Campaigning in Britain,* 1984, Heinemann Educational.

  Des Wilson has an impressive record as a lobbyist and was the Director of Shelter, which campaigned for the homeless. He was also heavily involved with the Child Poverty Action Group and the National Council for Civil Liberties, Friends of the Earth and Chair of the Committee for Freedom of Information. He also launched The Campaign for Lead Free Air (CLEAR), which took only 15 months to get ministers to decide to phase lead out of petrol.

  This and *Campaigning,* a similar book by him (Wilson, D with Leighton, A, 1993, Hawkesmere), contain a lot to inspire people to do likewise. However, there is a bias to assuming one will have a big organisation, with full time staff, which was his experience, but is not universal. The practical advice is rather general and dispersed through the books. There is little reference to sources of information and additional help. The books are also a little dated. Nonetheless, these are definitely the most interesting of the 'how to' books from a motivational standpoint.

- Watson, C, Ó Cadhla, M and Ní Dhurcáin, C, *Campaigns and How to Win Them,* 1997, Wolfhound.

  The authors have all been involved with Greenpeace and Irish environmental campaigns. The book attempts to give practical advice, but tends to assume a large organisation is necessary. It does try to give practical advice, for example, on how to run meetings, but fails to give enough information on any one thing to be really useful. Much of the book is directed at the situation in the Republic of Ireland and this is confusing to a reader in Britain, since much is simply inapplicable.

• Lattimer, M, *The Campaigning Handbook*, 1994, Directory of Social Change.

This is a very interesting book, covering many aspects of lobbying and containing case studies. It is now a little dated (no internet references, etc) and is biased towards the larger organisation, but has clear discussion of the issues involved. It is good on ways of setting up as a pressure group. It is by far the best of the 'how to' books for practical advice.

BOOKS BY PROFESSIONAL LOBBYISTS ABOUT THE PROFESSION OF LOBBYIST AND DIRECTORIES OF LOBBYISTS

These give an interesting insight into the world of the paid lobbyist. However, perhaps in the interest of maintaining professional mystique, they are unhelpful in explaining how to do it yourself.

• Souza, C, *So You Want To Be A Lobbyist? – The Inside Story of the Political Lobbying Industry*, 1998, Politico's.

This provides chatty views on lobbyists and the world of lobbying, but no practical advice and little help in any other way.

• Greer, J, *One Man's Word*, 1997, André Deutsch.

Ian Greer was the lobbyist at the centre of the cash for questions scandal and this is his own account of that episode and his career. Short on both practical advice and concrete achievements.

• Souza, C and Dale, I, *Directory of Political Lobbying*, 1999, Politico's.

A guide by way of lists and comments on professional lobbyists, lobbying firms and their connections with MPs. Contains a great deal of information if one wishes to hire a lobbyist or understand who is working for whom, but not a 'how to' book.

• Flower, J, *PMS Guide to Pressure Groups*, Issue No 3, 2000, Parliamentary Monitoring Services.

This is a list of pressure groups from Age Concern to the Wildlife Trust, giving brief details of what they do, their budget and who to contact there. Similar brief details are given of think tanks, political parties and groupings and professional lobbyists. A useful telephone directory style list, but not one trying to give any guidance on what to do.

SOCIOLOGICAL/POLITICAL BOOKS

These have the merit of giving a theoretical perspective on the process of lobbying for change. Practical books on how to lobby tend to be influenced only by the personal experience of the lobbyist. Lobbyists with permanent jobs in national campaigns tend to see this as the proper format for a campaign; others with experience of different types of campaigns see the small scale campaign as the norm.

The sociological/political perspective covers and classifies all the different types of campaigns and campaigners and gives a necessary overview of the field covered by pressure groups. The disadvantage is that there is no practical advice.

* Simpson, D, *Pressure Groups*, 1999, Hodder & Stoughton.

  A book designed for A level students of politics. An excellent, succinct summary of pressure groups and how they operate. Summarises and classifies the existing theories about the place and effectiveness of pressure groups in the political system. Bang up to date, but with no practical advice.

* Grant, W, *Pressure Groups, Politics and Democracy in Britain*, 2nd edn, 1995, Harvester Wheatsheaf.

  Another book at university undergraduate level on the theory of how pressure groups work. Less clearly structured than David Simpson's book and with no practical advice.

SOURCES OF INFORMATION

WEBSITES

Government Information site

www.open.gov.uk

This has links to a vast array of sites and contains a great deal of information.

Campaign for Freedom of Information site

www.cfoi.org.uk

Interesting in itself and for its links to other useful sites.

European Parliament site

www.europarl.eu.int

A lot of information can be found on this site, which is not as well constructed or easy to navigate as it might be.

Houses of Parliament site

www.parliament.uk

A vast resource of information.

LOBBYING IN EUROPE

Part of my campaign had always been the abolition of barriers to UK notaries getting work in Europe. The same principles applied, that is, analysing the problem, working out the vantage point and arguments of all the players and finding out who should be helping me and getting them to do so.

THE BACKGROUND

As explained in Chapter 2, the notarial profession is not an important one in the UK, but a central one in continental Europe. Continental notaries were often very rich indeed, due to the fact that:

- their numbers were generally limited by the State;
- they had an effective monopoly over many vital matters, for example, the transfer of property, the making of wills and the setting up of companies;
- they charged scale fees according to the value of the property transferred, which basically meant no price competition;
- they had local monopolies, so that even if you were appointed a notary, you were the only one or one of a very few appointed for an entire area;
- foreigners were excluded from applying or competing, since to be a notary of any kind in France, for example, you had to be French, in Germany, German, etc.

I considered that all of these points could be challenged, but the simplest course, as with the Scriveners, would be to attack the weakest point, the requirement that any notarial act done, say in France, had to be done by a French person.

THE PLAYERS

The European Commission

I filed a complaint with the Commission on 30 September 1996. I did this by writing to the Commission departments (each known as Directorate General or DG, followed by its number). The relevant ones for me were DG IV (Competition) and DG XV (Internal Market). I decided to complain against all the States which, in my view, were breaking the rules of the EU. Complainants need a legitimate ground of complaint. Mine was and is that I wish to set up a multi-national, cross-border notarial practice which can operate in every EU country.

Strict limits on how many notaries can be appointed, local monopolies and bans on foreigners entering the profession make such an aim impossible to achieve. I therefore had good grounds to complain and my case was duly allocated all the file numbers applicable. I also wrote to the heads of government of the Member States concerned, warning them of my claim and mentioning the probability that they, like the UK in the case of the Spanish fishermen (see p 25) would be liable to pay *Francovich* damages.

To recap, these are payable by a Member State if an individual or group of persons can show that they have suffered loss because of that State's failure to correctly implement binding provisions of EU law.

My argument was that:

- the anti-competition provisions of the EU Treaty outlawed local monopolies, limits on numbers of notaries appointed and scale fees;
- the free movement provisions of the EU Treaty made nationality conditions illegal. You could require that notaries were citizens of at least one EU State, but you could not insist they were nationals of your own country.

As with any other bureaucracy, the problem with the Commission was too many files and too few people to deal with them. The tendency is therefore to delay action and/or to push responsibility to other departments.

I noted immediately that DG IV wanted to avoid any liability for the file. They did not actually have the gall to say that none of the matters I had raised were breaches of competition rules (although they came very close), but said that so long as there was a nationality condition, it was not appropriate to take action on competition grounds – DG XV should act.

I disagreed with this and said so in writing. On the other hand, rejection of my case by DG IV was a kind of victory, since they too would be pushing DG XV to deal with my file. Pressure from inside your own organisation can be very strong, especially if the file can become an embarrassing one.

As with the UK Civil Service, the Commission is there to ensure the smooth running of the system. The difficulty is prioritisation and my means of pushing matters to the foreground would be insistence on compliance with EU law. Ultimately, no one could defend the current notarial set up and still proclaim the wonders of European unification and the Single Market.

To probe the Commission to act, I would therefore use:

- members of the European Parliament, who could ask questions the Commission would have to answer;
- the UK Civil Service, who, I was sure, had someone, somewhere whose duty it was to help me, a potential UK exporter;
- if necessary, UK MPs from the Commons, to embarrass the government as to why it was not helping me;
- the fear of adverse publicity, the ridicule arising from failure to get rid of such obviously unfair restrictions on competition.

The notarial professions

The English notarial profession had never seemed to take any interest in campaigning for the right of English notaries to set up shop in the EU. I determined to end this. The first step was making sure that foreign notaries could work here (described in Chapter 3). I reasoned that even those who had no desire to work in the EU would resent a situation in which foreign notaries could work here, when UK notaries could not work there.

I was constantly on the look out for potential allies. I found one in a fellow notary-to-be, Gregory Taylor, on the morning we were to sit the exams to become a notary. He had an interest in becoming a German notary, I discovered. I noted his number and kept in contact.

Matters came to a boil after we had won the Scrivener campaign. At a continuing professional education seminar for notaries in London in the spring of 1999, a large number of notaries were gathered. The end of the session left space for questions and answers to be put to the leading English notaries. I asked why we were not pushing for work opportunities in the EU, when every EU notary could work here.

I stressed what we all knew – other EU notaries earned fortunes, we earned very little. The gathering took my point and Gregory Taylor worked with the Notaries' Society and Hans Hartwig to organise a poll of all members as to whether the Notaries' Society should take up the case with the Commission. The poll resulted in many calls for action. Hans Hartwig, a key figure in the Scrivener struggle and a member of the ruling body of the Notaries' Society, was instrumental in making sure that the letter actually got sent to the Commission. It was only sent in the summer of 2000, but meant that there was an entire notarial profession now asking for free movement of notaries, not just me.

As with the Law Society in the Scrivener struggle, I was not concerned as to whether support was grudging or not, and whether the Notaries' Society had finally been converted to expansionism, or simply was afraid of losing its members' support. I simply needed the result and the letter.

The foreign notarial professions would be unlikely to support me. I decided simply to get them to explain why they would not allow migrants like me to practise. By sending a lot of faxes, I managed to boil down their argument to the essential, which was:

- I could not act as a notary of any type in France unless I became French first;

- they were justified in excluding me because they exercised 'official authority' (as discussed on pp 41–42);

- they were not keen to elaborate on exactly how they exercised this authority. Their arguments were always of the one or two sentence variety.

Luckily for me, notaries had themselves thought and written about the nature of their work and about the official authority argument. I decided to acquire their writings. As with the Scriveners, the most devastating arguments are always your opponents' own words.

The UK Civil Service

I wanted UK Government backing. I found out the name of the Minister for Trade and Industry and rang his Private Secretary at the DTI. He put me in touch with the department of the DTI which was responsible for ensuring a level playing field for UK companies seeking to export goods or services to the EU. That department was Action Single Market, at the DTI at Kingsgate House, 66–74 Victoria Street, London SW1.

I contacted them and wrote a summary of my case. We met and Jonathan Dennison Cross, who heads the department, and Nicola McLaughlin, who ably assists him, agreed to help me. They would write to the Commission to ask them to act. They had managed to get the Commission to persuade France to legislate to end the monopoly enjoyed by French licensed auctioneers and were interested in my case, where similar arguments were used in defence of the monopoly, and foreigners could not compete.

The Law Society

The Law Society were unwilling to help me, despite repeated requests and despite the fact that they told me they supported me. They did not want to create a fuss.

THE ARGUMENTS

I decided to research the arguments my adversaries would make as thoroughly as possible. I read all the existing cases relating to the 'official authority' argument, together with the case law of the ECJ on free movement and exceptions to it. These cases all stressed the difficulty of proving the 'official authority' defence. Crucially, the ECJ had even held that, even if you could prove that you did exercise such authority, you could not necessarily exclude foreigners. You needed to be able to prove that no measure short of excluding foreigners would protect the public from harm. Since the whole point of mutual recognition of qualifications was that notaries were already highly qualified in the law of their own State and would be required to take exams in the law of any state they moved to, the protection of the public was assured.

I used electronic search media to help. A CD ROM containing materials on EU that I consulted one Saturday at Westminster Public Reference Library showed that the Commission had already called on notaries to drop the nationality condition as incompatible with the EU Treaty and specifically Directive 89/48, the very point I had always argued.

PUSHING FOR VICTORY

I kept the European campaign ticking over throughout the Scrivener campaign. I then decided to push for the win and filed a complaint against the Commission for inaction with regard to my file on 13 September 1999. I copied that letter to all the various levels of DG XV (which I found detailed in *Vacher's European Companion*, published quarterly by Vacher Dod Publishing Ltd) and to Romano Prodi, President of the Commission. I said that matters had gone on long enough without action and that I would be asking for a public inquiry.

I heard back from the head of DG XV in a letter dated 6 October, but received by me on the 15 October 1999. I wrote back the next day. His department had suggested that I should sue the notaries myself. I had replied that this was the job of the Commission. Interestingly, he said that letters had been sent 'a little while ago' to the EU countries which imposed a nationality condition, asking for their explanation of why this was considered necessary.

In short, the file was now open and active. I contacted my MEPs (found on the European Parliament website) and asked them to support me. I got active support from Conservative MEPs Dr Charles Tannock and John Bowis, Labour MEP Robert Evans and the relevant Liberal Democrat and Green MEPs. I asked the various MEPs to do different things for me, both asking questions in the European Parliament and sending copies of my letters to the Commission and to the French Government.

Charles Tannock MEP was particularly helpful in getting (via the UK ambassador to Paris) a reply which made it clear that the only case which the French considered was a case of official authority was one in which a contract for a certain and specific money debt could be enforced against a debtor if he or she had signed the contract before a notary. Since this represented only a tiny percentage of all notarial work, it meant that the notaries' defence was even less arguable.

Robert Evans got replies to other queries and raised the issue of possible indirect discrimination caused by the fact that notarial practices tended, at least in France and Belgium, to be passed to nominees of the retiring notary. This meant that a lot of notarial practices were passed down through the family, from father to son.

PETITION TO THE EUROPEAN PARLIAMENT

I petitioned the European Parliament on the issue. You can do this via their website, details of which are in Appendix 6. I also complained to the European Ombudsman, again via a link on the European Parliament website. Although the Ombudsman rejected my complaint (presumably because I was now getting action from the Commission), I wanted to cover all options.

The petition had just been reviewed at the time of writing and the Petitions Committee had decided to refer the matter to the Commission. This again was helpful, since it meant another letter on the desk of the Commission asking what action was to be taken. In my situation, all publicity was good publicity.

WINNING THE ARGUMENT

I submitted some 40 pages of legal argument, backed up by extensive extracts from French and notarially authored books on law and notaries. Crucially, I found quotes from two notary authors which stated categorically that the notary had a duty not to impose his will on those who came to see him or her. The function of the notary was to carry out the intentions of the parties, putting them in legal form.

I agreed with this, but the admission was fatal to the notaries' case. Official authority, as exercised by a general or a judge, and as defined by the ECJ, was a power to coerce people to do things they did not want to do. Notaries did not have it.

I kept in close contact with the Commission official responsible for the file. Protocol and secrecy restrict what can be divulged, but I knew that the notaries only had official authority as an argument. Italy, Portugal and Spain indicated early on that they were willing to drop the nationality requirement. This was heartening for me and the Commission. Seven States, however, indicated that they would fight the case all the way to the ECJ. This would mean that the Commission would be suing seven countries, a larger number at one time on one issue than I had ever heard of.

VICTORY – STAGE ONE

The Commission decided to take the first stage of the enforcement procedure to abolish nationality requirements on 11 October 2000. The battle continues, but I think the result will be complete abolition of the restrictions I am fighting against.

INDEX